"TURNIP" TOWNSHEND

Statesman & Farmer

Susanna Wade Martins

Poppyland
Publishing

Front cover: Portrait of Charles, second Viscount Townshend by Sir Geoffrey Kneller. (By kind permission, Lord Townshend.)

© Susanna Wade Martins
ISBN 0 946148 46 5
Published by Poppyland Publishing, North Walsham, Norfolk
1990
Designed by Top Floor Design, Norwich
Printed by Printing Services (Norwich) Ltd
Typeset by PTPS, Norwich
Printed in Great Britain

Acknowledgements

I would like to thank the following people who have been very helpful in the writing of this book.

Viscount Townshend generously permitted me to study the documents at Raynham Hall and his secretary, Jane Kilvert, was often able to locate particular ones from the library and provide comfortable working conditions for me. Paul Rutledge of the Norfolk Record Office introduced me to the documents and has give valuable advice throughout the project.

Professor J M Rosenheim kindly allowed me to see the text of his major work on the first and second Viscounts Townshend, before its publication in the United States of America, and I am very grateful indeed for this privilege. Professor J R Jones of the University of East Anglia has read and made many helpful comments on my text.

The drawings are the work of Philip Judge.

Susanna Wade Martins
North Elmham
Norfolk
1990

"Turnip" Townshend

Statesman and Farmer

The life and times of Charles Townshend; born 1674; inherited the Raynham estate, Norfolk, and title of second Viscount, 1687; Privy Councillor, 1707; Ambassador Extraordinary to the States of Holland, 1709–1711; Secretary of State and Lord President of the Council, 1714–1716 and 1720–1730; died 1738.

"The importance of embassies, garters, vice-royalties and seals is as transitory as that of personal beauty; and the memory of this lord, though a man of great ability, will in a few ages be lost as a minister and a statesman and preserved only as a farmer."

Arthur Young of Townshend in the Annals of Agriculture (1786).

Contents

Townshend's Norfolk 7

The Townshend Inheritance 16

The Early Years 28

Return to Power... 41

The Years of Achievement 54

Townshend the Farmer 79

Townshend the Man.. 88

The avenue to the west front of Raynham Hall.

Townshend's Norfolk

The Norfolk into which Charles Townshend was born in 1674 was a county enjoying the peace and prosperity of the post-Restoration England of Charles II; his accession to the title of second Viscount and to the estates of Raynham came in the months after the birth of an heir to the Catholic king, James II. The Protestant fear that a Catholic line of monarchs would be established led to the much acclaimed "Glorious Revolution" of 1688 when the Catholic and absolute line was removed in favour of a Protestant constitutional monarchy.

Fears that England might again be plunged into the horrors of civil war proved to be unfounded and instead there was a peaceful transfer of power to William and Mary. By the time Charles died in 1738 a system of a parliamentary monarchy was in the process of development with power becoming centred in a cabinet presided over by a chief minister to whom the title of prime minister was becoming attached.

Agriculture too, Townshend's great interest outside politics, had moved on. The farming of his estates had finally changed from a medieval open-field system to the new Norfolk husbandry. It is these two strands of his life, played out by Townshend on his Norfolk estates and in the courts of Europe, that this book will follow.

Townshend's life may have spanned great agricultural and constitutional changes, yet some aspects of society remained remarkably stable. The "Glorious Revolution" consolidated the influence of the land owning gentry and aristocracy. After 1714, the Whigs established a permanent hold on office and power. There were few new faces amongst the great families of Norfolk. The "Glorious Revolution" had seen the Whig gentry triumph over the Catholic and Tory nobles and it was not until the late eighteenth century that merchants and lawyers began to find their way into the House of Commons and positions of power. Norfolk had not been dominated by a court connection since the downfall of the Duke of Norfolk in 1572. This had left a power vacuum from which many of the county's gentry had gained. The Townshends had bought land and with it increased their influence in north-west Norfolk. Although the Duke of Norfolk was reinstated in 1604, and again took on his traditional role at the head of the county as Lord

Lieutenant, he never regained the basis of his power. Finally in 1661 Charles' father, Horatio Townshend, replaced him in this prestigious position.

The Norfolk families who were well established by the end of the seventeenth century were the Townshends of Raynham, the Wodehouses of Kimberley, the De Greys of Merton, the Astleys of Melton Constable, the Cokes of Holkham, and the Windhams of Felbrigg. Slightly below them came the Harbords of Gunton, the Bacons of Stiffkey, the Buxtons of Heydon and the Walpoles of Houghton. The importance of the Pastons, so long influential in county affairs had declined by 1700. As a Catholic family they were excluded from office. The family seat at Oxnead Hall was sold in 1731 and was said to be a ruin by 1744. There were no newcomers to this dominant group in the eighteenth century and the surge of land prices and sales in the 1720s enabled the consolidation of the established gentry's position.

Grain prices, which had been low, began to rise in the early eighteenth century, and families who had felt the strain of a long period of low prices, coupled with the long-term effects of indebtedness resulting from the Civil War, took the opportunity offered by a more buoyant land market to sell out, mainly to the

The Great houses of early eighteenth century Norfolk

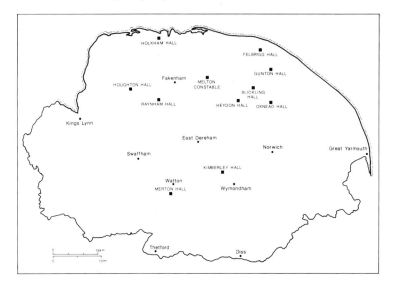

already powerful families. The Townshends and the Walpoles between them came to dominate both local and national politics within the county. The independent role of the gentry declined as a single well organised Whig ascendancy led by Townshend and Walpole rose to power. There were only six years between 1715 and 1796 when a Member of Parliament for Yarmouth was not a Townshend and five between 1702 and 1832 when a member for Kings Lynn was not a Walpole.

At a national level a peerage of about 160 formed an exclusive elite. "From some eighteenth century memoirs one might suppose that England was a federation of country houses." The political system within which Townshend operated has been described as "influenced by the smallness of the population, the difficulty of communication and the prevalence of disease." George I of Hanover inherited in 1714 and made short but frequent visits to Germany, taking the German members of his court and some close advisers with him, whilst the remaining ministers conducted the government's business in London. It was difficult for ministers to decide whether to stay in London or go with the king to Hanover would be more advantageous to their political careers.

Although the peers could not themselves sit in the House of Commons, they controlled the election of those who did. In Norfolk, there were two parliamentary places for the county as well as two each for the boroughs of Norwich, Great Yarmouth, Kings Lynn, Thetford and the tiny village of Castle Rising. The elections at Thetford and at Castle Rising were controlled by the Duke of Norfolk, although by the early eighteenth century both the Walpoles of Houghton and the Hostes of Sandringham owned properties·with voting rights in Castle Rising. As competition between rival families rose, so did the price of these properties. In the 1690s, the price of a cottage with voting rights in Castle Rising rose from £30 to £300. Traditionally, the two county seats had been controlled by the greatest landowners in the county. The lesser gentry felt that the magnates had influence and were therefore best placed to protect the gentry interests and so supported their candidates.

The towns had, however, been more independent, and seventeenth century Lynn had been represented by the merchants who lived there, but all this changed by the early eighteenth century. In acknowledgement of their support, members of the government and of Parliament gave detailed attention to local affairs and local appointments. "One man's sense of disappointment might change the delicate political balance of a neighbourhood."

There was no central supervision or control over local government and in the countryside the Lord Lieutenant was the most important position. The appointment was made by the Crown and so had political overtones meaning that the complexion of the government would be reflected in the countryside. The post was held by Charles Townshend's father, Horatio, from 1661 to 1675, and by Charles from 1701 to 1713 and 1714 to 1730. The Lord Lieutenant was the county's spokesman at Court and so was able to sit in the centre of the web of local patronage on which the exercise of local influence was based.

Below the Lord Lieutenant were the local Justices of the Peace, appointed by the Lord Chancellor and drawn from the gentry. Their duties increased during the eighteenth century, yet the position was a much coveted status symbol, sought after by the aspiring county gentry. JPs exercised a bewildering variety of functions. From the mundane tasks of dealing with vagrancy and drunkenness, they could, by the late eighteenth century, sentence a man to seven years transportation for rick burning. More serious offences would be heard by Justices acting together at Quarter Sessions. Other than their law enforcement duties, they could be law makers, regulating fairs and keeping the peace. They would appoint the constables for the ancient county divisions known as "Hundreds" who were then responsible for law and order within their areas. Finally, they administered the laws for such duties as repairing roads, licensing ale houses and certain aspects of the poor laws. The work involved was thought worthwhile in return for the local standing which the post engendered.

A county position shunned rather than sought after was that of Sheriff. By this date it was unimportant, except in election years when the sheriff acted as the returning officer. However, he did

Felbrigg Hall was built by Thomas Windham about 1620 and was amongst the lesser Jacobean mansions visited by early eighteenth century travellers (Below right) (Courtesy Royal Commission on the Historical Monuments of England)

Blickling Hall, the home of the Hobarts, was built between 1616 and 1627 and was one of the largest and most important houses in Norfolk in 1700 (above) (Courtesy Royal Commission on the Historical Monuments of England)

have the duty of entertaining the visiting assize judges every year, which made it a very expensive office to hold.

At the centre of each of the spheres of influence stood the country seat. The house was a symbol of the family's greatness and also the administrative centre of the estates and the many different enterprises included in them. The largest and most important houses in Norfolk in 1700 were Raynham, Blickling and Oxnead, although Oxnead, the home of the Paston family, was already in decline. Blickling, built between 1616 and 1627 for Sir Henry Hobart, Lord Chief Justice to James I, was designed by Robert Lyminge, the architect for Hatfield House 12 years before. The family had lost much of its influence by the early eighteenth century, although they later rose high after 1714, under the Georges. The style of the house was out of fashion in the 1700s and was generally described by visitors as "a bad old house". Raynham, although built at the same time as Blickling, was better appreciated. Although the design was much influenced by the houses of Inigo Jones, it was the work of Roger Townshend, himself an amateur architect. Roger sent his mason William Edge abroad, probably to the Low Countries, to study architecture and gather ideas. Together they worked out the final plans. Building probably began in 1622 and was completed 10 years later. Other houses visited by early eighteenth century travellers were Oxburgh and Melton Constable, the homes of the Bedingfields and the Astleys, with the lesser Tudor and Jacobean mansions of Heydon, Barningham and Felbrigg sometimes included.

Townshend's Norfolk looked very different to that of the present day. Not only were the most impressive buildings, after the churches, the fine country houses surrounded by their formal gardens which were later enlarged into great parks, but much of this prosperous countryside remained unenclosed and hedgeless into the eighteenth century. Between the open fields were large areas of heath and common. Although there had been much consolidation in the open fields, and few farmers still farmed scattered strips, much of the commons remained open sheep walk, particularly on the light lands around Raynham. The consolidation of strips and the enclosing of them by tenant farmers meant that the right of the landlord to graze his sheep over the open fields after harvest (the right of shackage) was gradually being eroded and with it the domination of sheep farming by landlords. In the sixteenth century,

The late Elizabethan house at Heydon was built by Henry Dynne, one of the auditors of the Exchequer and was popular with early eighteenth century sight-seers (above) (Courtesy Royal Commission on the Historical Monuments of England)

Stiffkey Hall, set in the watermeadows beside the river Glaven and the church was the home of the 16c. Nathaniel Bacon whose daughter married Roger Townshend, the builder of Raynham and so Stiffkey and its surrounding lands became part of the Raynham estate. (Below) (Courtesy Royal Commission on the Historical Monuments of England).

13

the Townshends had prospered by large-scale sheep farming, rather than letting their land, but by the late seventeenth century income from tenant farms was more important.

The crops being grown had begun to change by the time of Charles Townshend's birth. From the 1650s, agricultural writers were advocating the growing of turnips and selected clovers for winter feed and improved hay and pasture. The nitrogen rich clover seems to have been more widely grown and from an earlier date, than turnips which were not generally cultivated before 1680. Turnips were grown at Raynham by 1690, and inventory evidence suggests they were grown on up to 50 per cent of Norfolk farms by 1710, although only in small quantities. The turnip had long been grown as a field crop in the intensively farmed Low Countries and some farmers sent their sons to Holland to learn new methods. The idea of cultivating turnips as a winter fodder crop for livestock undoubtedly came from there. They were autumn sown and this precluded the opening of the fields for winter shackage. While some landlords tried to fight this development, others realised that the cultivation of turnips might well result in a better winter feed and accepted the change as inevitable. With the end of shackage for the landlords' flocks, the last remaining advantage of open fields was gone and so tenant farms were further reorganised into compact holdings with hedged fields allowing tenants as well as landlords to keep sheep. Sheep were kept mainly on the open heaths in summer and folded on the turnip fields in winter, and this remained the basis of Norfolk husbandry into the eighteenth century.

Weaving was Norwich's main industry. The city had recovered from the depression of the sixteenth century with the introduction of the "new draperies" from Holland. After 1600 these were known as "Norwich Stuffs" and produced by Norwich weavers. Visitors to the city commented, not on its poverty, as had been the case earlier, but on its prosperity, cleanliness and the number of gardens.

Spinning and knitting continued to be the basis of non-agricultural employment in the countryside. Celia Fiennes writing in the late seventeenth century commented, "the county is full of spinners and knitters" and Daniel Defoe in 1722, praised the fact that "there is not any hand unemployed, if they want work; and the very children over four or five years of age, could every one earn their own bread." The prosperity of the county depended very much on the cloth trade, and when fashions changed and imports, particularly calicoes, were being worn Townshend was under great pressure from his supporters to enforce measures to protect the woollen weavers; these laws were passed in 1720 and 1721.

Norfolk was a prosperous and populous county with a flourishing economy based on agriculture and the producing of wool. The low price of grain meant that there was a surplus for export and much of this went through Kings Lynn and the north coast ports. Lynn's years of greatest prosperity were at the end of the seventeenth century. Its large hinterland covered much of eastern England and was connected to it by the river system of the Great Ouse. Grain was the main export, and coal a major import. Defoe described Lynn as "a beautiful, well built and well situated town." Like Norwich, Kings Lynn was ruled by a group of leading merchants, but they were susceptible to the influence of the neighbouring gentry. Some, like the Turners, bought country estates and many had connections with the leading county families such as the Townshends.

Although the fear of destitution and starvation was a spectre never far removed from the poor, Townshend's Norfolk was a county with an appearance of prosperity; fine gentry and yeoman houses in the countryside alongside busy market towns and ports. Wide open commons were grazed by the hardy and agile Norfolk sheep, and open fields were beginning to give way to hedged enclosures in which new crops from Holland could be grown. Its social and commercial focal point was the provincial capital and industrial centre of Norwich, but it also had close ties across the North Sea with Germany and the Low Countries. It relied for its link with London and the court on a small group of universally accepted leaders of whom the Townshend family were the foremost. This was the land and society that formed the backcloth to the people and events described in this book.

The Townshend Inheritance

Norfolk suffered less than many other counties as a result of the Civil War (1640-1649). Always a "self-contained province", isolated by the natural boundaries of rivers, Breckland and the sea, it had long been influenced by Puritan, Calvinist teachings from the Low Countries, and there were few risings in support of the king. During the Civil War, the Raynham estate was run by trustees for Sir Horatio Townshend who was a child at the time and so did not become involved, thus ensuring that the estate remained intact. When Horatio came of age, he showed definite Royalist leanings and worked hard to influence puritanical Norfolk in favour of the king's return. In 1660 he was one of 12 commissioners entrusted by Parliament with the message inviting the king back. He was made a lord at the Restoration, when the family's connection with the Court began. In 1661 Lord Townshend was made Lord Lieutenant of Norfolk and used his very considerable influence and patronage to gain the support of the leading families in the county for the restored monarchy. In 1667 Charles II stayed at Raynham and when Horatio's first son was born in 1674, he was christened Charles in honour of the king who, with the Duke of York, was a godparent. In 1682, Horatio was finally rewarded with the title of Viscount Townshend of Raynham. When Horatio died in 1687, Charles inherited not only a title, but the essentials for a successful political career at the end of the seventeenth century: connections at Court and respect in the County.

Charles also inherited extensive estates amounting to over 15000 acres making him one of Norfolk's largest landowners alongside his near neighbours at Holkham and Houghton. These possessions produced a rent of about £3300. The largest amount was derived from the three Raynham parishes with his various Suffolk possessions second in importance and much smaller sums coming from the other Norfolk parishes. Much of the estate was around the family seat at Raynham, but a second group of parishes on the north coast, including Stiffkey, Langham and Morston, had come to the Townshend family, through marriage, from the Bacons of Stiffkey. Finally there were the outlying estates such as the village of Shipdham, a large parish about 18 miles to the south, where he was lord of the manor and owned three farms.

The villages of Pattesley, Oxwick, Toftrees and Shereford were all near Raynham and had all shrunk in size since the Middle Ages. Ruined or isolated churches are all that remain of several of them. At Pattesley the only evidence for the church is an arch built into the farmhouse and Oxwick church is a ruin. At Coxford there is part of a priory, while at Toftrees, the church stands alone, presumably near the site of its long abandoned village. Examples such as these demonstrate the dramatic decline in the population of Norfolk in the 100 years after the Black Death of 1348 which enabled landlords such as the Townshends to take more land in hand and run huge flocks of sheep thus laying the foundations of their family wealth. By 1700, the parishes of Pattesley, Toftrees and Shereford were each let as single farms, while Lord Townshend kept his own flock of about 200 wethers at Coxford with ewes at Rudham and South Creake and flocks of wethers at Stiffkey and on Rudham "great ground".

Map showing the Norfolk estates of Charles second Viscount Townshend

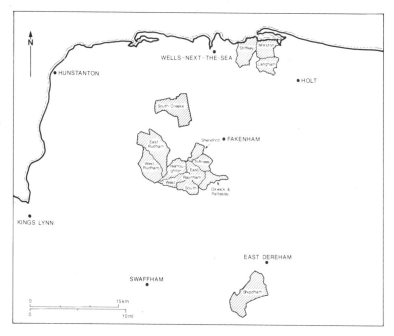

Toftrees church and one farm are all that remain of the medieval village of Toftrees

The ruins of Coxford Abbey are still surrounded by low-lying meadows used for sheep grazing

Not all the villages within the parishes of the estate were decayed. East and West Rudham and Helhoughton were more populous, and Lord Townshend owned and let both large farms and small pieces of land here as well as keeping his own sheep on the commons.

By far the largest numbers of tenants were to be found in the three Raynham parishes. There were two large farms in East Raynham, both held on life leases in 1700, two in West Raynham and one in South Raynham as well as 30 or so small tenants.

Unlike the depopulated area around Raynham, the coastal villages of Langham, Morston and Stiffkey were thriving fishing and trading ports, with about eight farms of over 30 acres, one of which was over 300, and nearly 50 tenants of houses or small pieces of land. Stiffkey Hall, the fine sixteenth century mansion built by Nathaniel Bacon was also let as a farm house by 1700 and had long ceased to be a seat of the family.

Plans of several of the Townshend parishes were drawn in the early sixteenth century and from these (pp20–21) it is possible to reconstruct their appearance at the time. West Raynham village had two nuclei, roughly where the settlement is today; one at the crossroads near the church where about a dozen houses are shown, and a second smaller one to the west along the "Common Drove-way" which widens out to the west to form the "old heath", and finally, beyond Kipton and Cannon's Green there are the "lyngs" which border onto Helhoughton common. To the north of the church was a moat, presumably the site of an old manor house and no longer occupied. There is no sign of it today. To the south and west the village was surrounded by strip fields, while to the north, around the moated site the fields were larger enclosures.

Settlement at East Raynham was much more scattered, but still roughly where it is now, clustered at the entrance to the Park near the church, and to the east, on what is now the main road, but was then a small common. A third scattering of houses was further west again, on the way to Oxwick along the edge of a common, but all this has disappeared. Between the commons are the open fields, with larger enclosures only found near the Hall where the formal rectangular Dutch-style gardens are shown. On the area of common bordering on the parish of Toftrees a shepherd with his flock is drawn, indicating the most important use for this area.

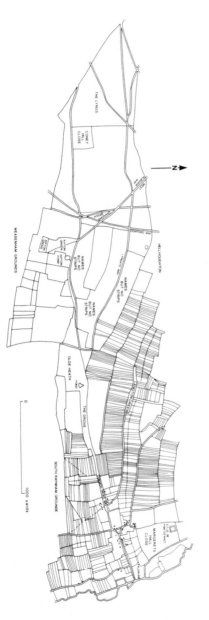

Map of West Raynham in 1620 showing the strip fields to the east and to the west, more distant from the village, the large areas of open common (left)

Map of East Raynham in 1620 showing strip fields, scattered settlements, small areas of common and the formal gardens beside the Hall (right).

The large area of commons in the north of East Raynham parish carried on into Helhoughton and a further long finger into East Rudham. Both of these were populous villages in the 1630s. At Helhoughton, houses are strung out along a lane running south from the church towards West Raynham. There are only a few houses along this stretch now, at the Helhoughton end; the rest of the lane is no more than a footpath. The houses were all on the west

21

side of the road, with their strip fields behind and overlooking large enclosures, probably water meadows, between the street and the river. There were two larger farms with enclosed fields, to the west, one described as "the site of hall". The houses at East Rudham were mostly around a large green known as the Fairstead and Broadgate to the east. The most substantial group of buildings and also one of the farms that commanded the highest rent on the estate (£135 in 1696) was at the old Coxford Priory where Townshend kept a flock of sheep as well as letting the farm.

This map of East and West Raynham, drawn 100 years after the previous two, shows the area after most of the strips had disappeared, but while the commons still existed.

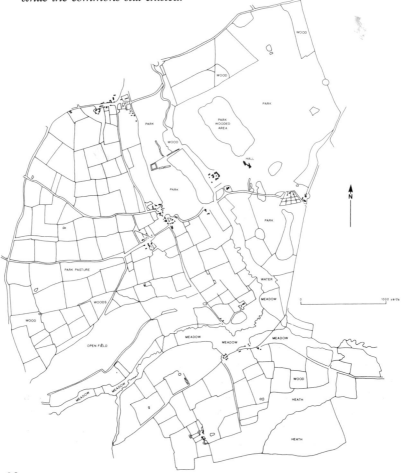

The lane linking Helhoughton and West Raynham is shown on the 17th century maps but has now disappeared for much of its length. A few houses still remain at the Helhoughton end, (above), and there is an indication in the gable end that this (left) cottage was far smaller, with a steeply pitched roof, probably dating from the seventeenth century.

These maps emphasise very clearly the organisation of settlement and agriculture at the time. Villages surrounded by their open fields were no more than oases within vast heaths and commons. That much of the land stayed this way into the time of Charles Townshend is shown in the rentals. In 1701, Thomas Burrage rented "79 acres of infield, 35 acres in three brecks of the great ground field in East and West Raynham." There were also several tenants renting land worth less than one pound, which must have been no more than a few strips in the open fields. Although there were more than 100 tenants on the Norfolk estate, not more than 20 were renting substantial holdings. The highest rent was £335 paid by Rudding for the whole of the parish of Toftrees, an area of over 1100 acres, much of it still open heath. Three other farmers were paying rent of over £250 in 1701 and these men must have been the elite of the farming community and the predecessors of the farmers of the huge light land farms so typical of north-west Norfolk a couple of generations later.

Some of the common land in Tatterset still survives and rough heathland such as this provided the grazing for the hardy Norfolk sheep kept about here in Townshend's time

Another type of rental paid was for fold courses. In earlier centuries a fold course had been the land allotted to one manor over which the lord could run his sheep, and as most Norfolk parishes contained more than one manor, most were divided into several fold courses. A fold course contained a variety of land to provide for the all-year grazing of the sheep. It would therefore include arable open fields for winter feeding (shackage), as well as open heath for the summer. Several of the tenants were renting fold courses which again suggests that the open fields were unenclosed. In 1701 Francis Hill paid £111 for "a farm, fold course, woods and closes" in Shereford. The existence of fold course rights over the fields shows that there was obviously much improvement waiting to be carried out on the Raynham estate. If the full benefit of the new turnip crop was to be felt, the fields needed to be enclosed and fold courses broken up to allow their cultivation.

When Charles Townshend inherited at the age of 13, guardians took over the running of the estate. As was frequently the case when an estate was run by trustees, it was managed extremely efficiently. Children were not as expensive to maintain as adults and so income from rents could be used to pay off debts or to build up capital. Charles was sent to Eton and Cambridge before completing his education with the Grand Tour between 1694 and 1698, costing about £1000 per annum. This prepared him for a place in seventeenth century cultured society, and he was always a politician who felt at home in any court in Europe. When Townshend came of age in 1698, he had an income of between £5000 and £6000 a year from an estate entirely unencumbered by debt, a rare and very fortunate situation in which to be.

At the centre of Charles Townshend's estates was the Hall, built by his grandfather, Sir Roger Townshend, between 1622 and 1632. The most important architect of the Court at the time was Inigo Jones who from 1615 was the Surveyor General of the King's Works and Buildings and so in fact fulfilled very few commissions beyond his work for the royal family. It was he who established the basic form for an elegant house as a simple cube, often with the addition of a triumphal arch motif as a centre piece and executed in red brick with stone detailing around doors, windows and at corners. Raynham is one of the earliest houses to be influenced by these ideas, possibly because its building followed closely on Inigo Jones' completion of the Prince's Lodgings at Newmarket in 1623.

This redrawing of the east and west fronts of Raynham Hall in 1671 shows the house as it was originally designed by Sir Roger. In both fronts there are two doors rather than the single one of today. The present doors were probably inserted about 1705 during a phase of alteration.

Sir Roger had no doubt watched progress there as he travelled to and from London and wished to emulate it in his new house. Raynham Hall was completed about 1632, but Sir Roger never lived there and the second Viscount inherited a house built in a style that was still considered very up-to-date and had been little altered since it was built. The present house however, is rather different to that of the 1660s. Plans drawn in 1671 show the original house had two doors in the west and east fronts rather than the single ones we see today. The door arrangement and some of the windows appear to have been altered by the time Edmund Prideaux visited and drew the house in the early eighteenth century, perhaps during a phase of building around 1705. At the end of the 1720s Charles Townshend commissioned the fashionable architect, William Kent, to alter the house again. Most of Kent's work was on the interior, so whilst it is mainly Sir Roger's work that we see externally, it is the second Viscount's inside. The largest room in the house is the Belisarius room, with its impressive ceiling, part of Sir Roger's original design. Unlike the rest of the state rooms, it is on the first floor, above the chapel, but was one that would certainly have been used to entertain eminent guests.

Charles Townshend's inheritance therefore included "standing" both in the County and Court, one of the most extensive and best managed estates in Norfolk, producing an income large enough to support his position, and a fine house of fashionable design in which to entertain. It certainly seemed that he had all the necessary prerequisites for a brilliant political career.

The saloon as redesigned by Kent with classical pediments over the doors and fire places (Copyright A F Kersting)

The Early Years

Charles Townshend was born in 1674, the first of the three sons of Horatio and his second wife, Mary, the daughter of Sir Joseph Ashe of Twickenham. Two other sons, Roger and Horatio, were born before she died of smallpox. Their father died when Charles was only 13, leaving the children orphans and in the charge of guardians, one of whom was Colonel Robert Walpole of Houghton. The Townshend and Walpole families were close neighbours and friends. Colonel Robert had six children; his eldest son, Robert, was two years younger than Charles and together they were to lead the Whig party in the reign of George I. Robert's younger brother Horace was also a close friend and loyal secretary to Charles in his early career, while Dorothy Walpole eventually became Charles's wife; a match that had long been contemplated but which had been disapproved of by Dorothy's father, Colonel Robert Walpole. According to Walpole's eighteenth century biographer, William Coxe, Robert refused to agree to the marriage "lest he should be suspected of forming a match so advantageous to his family by improper means." By the time the marriage (Townshend's second) took place, Robert was dead.

Charles and his brothers spent much time at Houghton; in those days a house far less grand, but not dissimilar to Raynham, built of red brick and finished in 1660. The two young families grew up together and the friendships and loyalties which affected so greatly their later lives developed.

The boys from both families went to Eton and Roger went on to become a lawyer before entering parliamant. A list of Charles' school expenses survives. Not only do they include the essential books, paper and ink, but equally important, quantities of ginger cake. Anne Newborough was the housekeeper in charge of the boys in the early 1690s and even then the streak of ill-temper which was so much part of Charles's character in later life, was apparent. Anne wrote to London in 1692, "I received all the young gentlemen's things and they fitt them very well, but my lord does not think his night gown good enough and therefore, if it can be changed, I will send it." Later his guardian, Thomas Calthorpe wrote, "My lord is very angry with the saddler for disappointing him so many times. Pray tell him to be once as good as his word for my lord will not be so dealed with."

The educating of the upper classes at school was by no means universal by the late seventeenth century. Many still remained at home with private tutors and the public schools were still catering for poorer boys, as their founders had intended. Gradually the practice of taking fee-paying boarders increased at the expense of the day boys, until their reputation as educational establishments for the wealthy of the land became established.

The education provided fitted sons of the aristocracy for a life of leisure and politics. It was based on a study of the classics and so was by no means utilitarian.

Portrait of Charles, second Viscount Townshend by Sir Godfrey Kneller (By kind permission, Lord Townshend)

From Eton, Charles Townshend went to Cambridge which was certainly the preserve of the upper classes. After spending a few years there, he left with "a reputation for learning" and set off on a European Tour in the manner of the sons of the aristocracy. His travelling companion and tutor was Dr William Sherard, an Oxford scholar with an interest in botany. We know very little about their movements and activities; in 1696 they were in Italy and they returned to England during 1697. £2723 10s 8d was paid by Charles' guardians to maintain him abroad.

The grand tour was an advantage which only the wealthy could afford, and so was the hallmark of an aristocratic education. On his travels the young man would learn something of the ways of his social equals across Europe, as well as develop a taste for the fashionable art and sculpture of France and both classical and contemporary Italy.

It was to this travelling that Charles owed the ability to speak and write fluent French and to be at ease in the courts of Europe. When Charles came of age in 1695, he came into an estate that had been very ably run by executors. Thomas Ward remained as steward until his death in 1710 and two other executors, Edward LeStrange and Thomas Calthorpe, continued to be valued advisers until their deaths in 1715 and 1717. Early correspondence shows that Towhshend took an interest in estate improvements such as enclosure and the planting of woodland, but as he became more involved in politics he had to leave more in the capable hands of his steward.

Immediately on his return from abroad he began to prepare the ground for his chosen career in politics. In 1697, at the age of 23, he took his seat in the House of Lords, although he did not speak in a debate until 1701. Although Charles' father supported Charles II, he could not go so far as to believe in the Divine Right of Kings, so this led him rather reluctantly to side with the Whigs after 1679. Charles' first speech was against the acquittal of three leading Whigs who had been impeached for corrupt practices in the setting up of the "new" East India Company, for massive bribery at general elections and the installation of partisan JPs. However, he soon changed his allegiance and joined the Whig group in the House of Lords.

The House of Lords which he entered was a very select and powerful body. There were only about 160 peers eligible to sit and

Portrait of Elizabeth Pelham, first wife of Charles Townshend, attributed to Sir Godfrey Kneller, 1723 (By kind permission, Lord Townshend)

of these, not more than two thirds were active members. On July 30th 1698 Charles married Elizabeth Pelham at the family home in Chelsea. Her father later became First Baron Pelham and this marriage brought Charles both a substantial dowry and relatives with political influence within the tight ruling class.

Redrawing of a sketch of the east front of Raynham Hall, by Edmund Prideaux made in the early 18th century showing the modern arrangement of doors already in existence before Kent's main period of work at Raynham.

In August 1699 the first of their many children was born. Although the family hardly ever spent more than half of the year at Raynham, the house became a family home again and in 1703 Townshend began a series of major alterations to the house. No plans survive to indicate what changes he was making, but drawings made about 1671 and 1720 show that the exterior of the house was changed considerably, quite probably in 1703–4. The replacement of the two separate doors on either side of the central block on both the east and west fronts by central entrances in both fronts must have involved major alterations to the internal arrangements as well. It is not surprising therefore that Townshend was put out by his brother's surprise decision to visit Raynham in 1703. He wrote, "I hear my brother, Horace, designs to come into Norfolk very suddenly. I should be very glad to see him here if I had any room to lodge him, but I protest that I have taken down so much of my house and have so many workmen in that part of it which is standing and furnished that I have at this time only two spare beds in all my house." The alterations were still incurring expense the following year when stone was needed to complete them. Although Townshend was prepared to see some estate improvement involving the relatively simple business of exchanging parcels of land to consolidate his possessions, he did not want to be committed to expense on the farms because of the work on the house.

When the family was living at Raynham, they still had contacts with London and there were certain goods that could only be supplied adequately from the capital. Snuff, tea and "Bristol water" were ordered through Mr Leamon at The Three Nuns in Fleet Street and sent to Norfolk either by the weekly waggons or the Kings Lynn coach. Clothes and suits were also made in London and sent up. Great consternation was caused when goods ordered did not arrive, and Lord Townshend's reputation for a quick temper is shown to be justified in this letter sent by his valet to Mr Leamon in October 1704. "This comes to acquaint you that either by misfortune or neglect, you have committed a great crime in not sending my lady's (lavither?) by the last carrier or the Lynn coach as you promised and being quite out, made my lord and lady so angry that they said more than I need repeat." Again on April 16th 1705, he wrote, "The last waggon coming without the chest of Florence which was impatiently expected, put my lord in a violent passion against you and therefore I beg you would take more care for the future and see things delivered yourself. I hope it will come this time or there will be mad work."

In most years at the beginning of the century, the family would spend the summer at Raynham, returning to London in October or November. The journey would take two or three days and was always uncomfortable. A letter from Raynham to Mr Leamon written on November 6th 1701 said, "My lord desires you to go to Mr Callow and with his assistance procure a very large, strong and easy coach with six stout and good horses and a careful coachman and postilion to be at Raynham on saturday next and to set out on the monday following for London, that coach being so designed for young children and nurses must be pretty roomy...and against wednesday night following you are desired to see that we have some hay and straw in my lord's stable made ready to receive the horses when they come." The journey from London to Raynham, a distance of about 120 miles, took three days with eight or nine stops. At the East Anglian end, these included Newmarket, Barton Mills, Brandon and Swaffham. Expenses for the journey in 1727 amounted to £25. Once back in London it was the web of family connections that was more important to advance in government than the political parties of modern times.

The two political parties that were to become more important in the reign of Queen Anne were the Whigs and the Tories. The Tories had supported the Stuarts and their belief in the Divine Right of Kings and were strong upholders of the Established Church, particularly against Presbyterianism. Their supporters included some of the oldest aristocratic families and those who feared the undermining of their privileges. It was the Whig element which supported the Protestant succession and so invited William and Mary; they orchestrated the signing of the Bill of Rights and the setting up of a constitutional monarchy in 1688. They were therefore strong supporters of the Hanoverian rather than the Stuart succession and branded the Tories as Jacobites.

Queen Anne inherited the throne from William III in 1702 and, initially, power went to the Tories who had sympathised with Anne in her conflicts with William in his final years. Many Whig seats in the House of Commons were lost in the 1701 election but the Whigs soon regained power. Their leadership was firmly rooted in a small group of five peers, or the "junta", working from their base in the House of Lords. These men not only controlled the voting of a large and loyal following in the upper house, but through their manipulation of patronage and elections to the Commons, commanded a disciplined and formidable group in the lower chamber as well.

Charles Townshend, like most other lords, had friends and influence in the Commons and from quite early in Anne's reign, the group who were to form Walpole's and Townshend's supporters could be seen beginning to form. Initially it was very much of a local group. Walpole followed his friend to Westminster in 1701, sitting for the family-controlled seat at the small town of Castle Rising which sent two MPs to parliament, in spite of having no more than 60 voters. Unlike Townshend, Walpole went to London with few friends in high places and relied on Townshend who acted very much as his guide and sponsor. From 1705 to 1710, Walpole was Secretary of War, and later held the lucrative post of Secretary to the Navy. John Holland of Quidenham, in South Norfolk, was another member of the group, an MP and Comptroller of the Household from 1709 to 1711. Walpole's brother-in-law, John Turner, an MP for Kings Lynn, was a Commissioner of Trade. Other local members of the group were Townshend's brother, Roger, an MP for Yarmouth and Walter Bacon and John Chambers, MPs for Norwich. It was these local loyalties based on neighbourliness and the sharing of common local interests which were important in holding groups together at Westminster.

Through Queen Anne's reign, the power of the House of Lords increased and all the important politicians of the reign were, or became, peers. The "junta" increased their influence within Queen Anne's cabinet during the early years of her reign. This was the first period in which ministers actually governed. Previously, William III had made all major policy decisions. Seats in the House of Lords were sought by commoners, not simply because of their social prestige, but because commoners knew that political power came more easily via that route.

Queen Anne's reign was dominated by war; both the very real war against France abroad and the fear of a disputed succession at the death of Anne. Before Anne could be sure of the necessary stability at home to fight with confidence abroad, the loyalty of Scotland to the Protestant Succession needed to be secured. Scotland was still virtually two nations, with the Highland Catholic clans to the north and west and the Lowland Presbyterians to the south. There were still many, mainly in the Highlands, who supported the Catholic Stuart line in the person of James III of England and VIII of Scotland, son of the exiled James II and VII and recognised as the rightful king of England and Scotland by Louis XIV, on the death of his father in 1701. Some were even prepared to see two kingdoms with separate monarchs again. In the 1690s the Club of Radicals led by Montgomery had proposed that James II should return to Scotland as king, but only if he agreed to concessions limiting his constitutional powers. Although England and Scotland had shared one monarch since 1603, they still had separate parliaments, and it was to achieve the total unity and thus, it was hoped, the loyalty, of Scotland, that the Act of Union, bringing to an end the Scottish parliament, was proposed. A first effort was made in 1703, but the stumbling block was the future position of the Scottish Presbyterian church. It was the refusal of the Scots to accept an episcopal system that had precipitated the Civil War against Charles I two generations previously and it was over their demands for assurances that negotiations broke down. Both sides realised the importance of reaching a settlement within Queen Anne's life-time and so after several trials of strength on both sides, discussions reopened in April 1706. These negotiations provided Charles Townshend with his first opportunity to show his diplomatic skills as a member of a 31-strong commission, most of them Whigs, set up to work out terms with the Scots. To achieve their political aims, the commission was prepared to make certain concessions, particularly in the field of free trade, creating a united market between Scotland and England and giving the Scots access to Britain's overseas colonies. However, Scotland was in a far weaker bargaining position, being a smaller and markedly poorer country with her traditional lines of trade with France, Holland and Scandinavia declining and dislocated by wars. The political system was corrupt and controlled by a small number of aristocrats who spent most of their time in London where, alongside the English lords, they were competing for patronage and influence.

By July the negotiators had agreed on the terms for an Act of Union. The separate system of Scottish law was to continue and the rights of the Scottish Presbyterians were to be guaranteed. This last concession was resented by the High Church Anglican Tories. The economic inducements of free access to English trade, markets and colonies along with the provision for reduced rates of taxation, because of the country's relative poverty, coupled with a certain amount of bribery, ensured that the Act was passed in both countries. The Scottish parliament came to an end and instead 45 MPs and 16 peers from Scotland went to Westminster.

It is not clear how far Townshend was responsible for the successful outcome of these negotiations, but in 1707, he was made Captain of the Yeoman of the Queen's Guard and as the Whig "junta" increased its hold on the government, he gained their recognition and a seat in the Privy Council, also in 1707. By 1709, there were four "junta" leaders in the Cabinet Council and when an ambassador was needed to go to The Hague to persuade the Dutch not to negotiate separately with the French, Townshend was recommended to accompany the Duke of Marlborough on this highly delicate mission. Townshend had been to Holland several times over the previous few years as a diplomat, all of which suggests that he had proved his abilities by playing a leading role in the negotiations with Scotland.

While Townshend had been preoccupied with Scottish affairs he had been kept closely in touch with the progress of the French war through a detailed correspondence with those involved on the battlefields of Europe. The fears of the countries that joined the "Grand Alliance" (Britain, Holland, Denmark, Austria, Prussia and Portugal) that the succession of the grandson of Louis XIV of France to the Spanish throne would lead to a Europe dominated by France and Spain had led to the outbreak of war in 1701. The Duke of Marlborough was leader of the British army and succeeded in pushing the French out of the Netherlands. He then raced to southern Germany where he fought and won the Battle of Blenheim in 1704. There followed a series of successes in France and the Netherlands, at Ramilles (1706), Oudenarde (1708) and Malplaquet (1709). France seemed near defeat. Within France, the decay of trade and industry during the wartime disruption, mounting taxation and the catastrophically severe winter of 1708-9 meant that the French were ready to seek peace at almost any price. In Britain too, there was war weariness and Anne began to suspect that Marlborough and her ministers were keeping the war going for their own purposes. The Dutch who relied on peace for the conduct of their trade, also wanted to see a negotiated peace, and in April 1709 Louis, seeing the Dutch as likely to be sympathetic to overtures for peace, sent Torcy, his foreign minister, to the Hague to try and negotiate terms.

There were three concessions that were required from Louis; firstly the Spanish throne must not be held by a French Bourbon, but by the Austrian Hapsburg claimant; secondly, both the vulnerable states of Holland and Savoy must have defensive barriers against French attack; and thirdly, Louis must accept the Protestant Hanoverian succession to the British throne and expel the Pretender James III from France. These were very harsh terms amounting to virtual capitulation and there was to be two months truce to allow for the final details of the peace to be worked out during which time key fortresses were to be handed over to the allies. Louis refused to accept these final conditions and so negotiations broke down. The Dutch were ready to make more concessions than the British and so to forestall this Townshend went with Marlborough to the Hague as "Ambassador Extraordinary" to try and negotiate a settlement acceptable to the Dutch. Townshend's appointment to this key position was sponsored by Baron Somers, now Lord Chancellor, and shows Townshend's growing standing with the Whig "junta". He was not the only member of the Norfolk group to gain new power; in 1709 Robert Walpole became Secretary of War and his brother, Horace, went with Townshend as his secretary.

Townshend's party also included his ever-increasing family. Five waggons were needed to transport "people and goods". Horses had to be hired and people and animals fed. Animals included not only his dogs which needed bread, but his chickens which ate corn. Finally, when the family returned in 1711, they disembarked at Yarmouth, but the animals went to Greenwich and had to be fetched from there. New Year was an expensive time for Townshend in Holland because both his personal staff, including the children's dancing and writing masters and the 20 servants, and the office staff, such as those who organised the postal services and the sexton of the English church, had to be given presents. In all the personal expenses incurred by this itinerant life in Holland

View of the Count Pond, near Binnehof, The Hague, by P C la Fargue in 1763; a scene that had probably changed little since Townshend was familiar with it 50 years previously (Copyright Collection Haags Gemeentemuseum)

amounted to about £3000.

The task facing Townshend in Holland was not an easy one. Although the Dutch and the British had a mutual interest in preventing the French domination of commercial outlets in Spain and the Spanish territories in South America and the Netherlands, they could not agree on how to split the spoils resulting from a successful conclusion of the war. The Dutch as a predominantly commercial people had suffered more than Britain during the war and felt the war aims had expanded beyond those which would benefit Holland. She seemed prepared to make her own peace with France and it was to prevent this that Townshend negotiated the Barrier Treaty. The resulting terms were very unpopular in Britain, as Townshend was thought to have paid too high a price for a guarantee of Dutch support for the Hanoverian succession. The Dutch were to have garrisoned fortresses in the Spanish Netherlands to provide an effective barrier against aggression. The agreement that at the end of the war the English and Dutch merchants would have an equal share in whatever advantages were gained in the Spanish colonies in South America brought complaints from the English merchants.

It would certainly seem that Townshend showed bad judgement in these negotiations and criticisms of the terms of the Barrier Treaty in England weakened the Whigs' negotiating position when the time came to move on to Geertentruidenberg to take part in the Dutch initiated peace talks with the French. Lord Townshend wrote to Horace Walpole who had returned briefly to England, "I am under a great deal of concern upon account of the difficulties the treaty for the barrier has met with in England, which has not a little increased the fits of spleen for which you have so often laughed at me. As to our evenings, you will easily believe we are in a very melancholy way of passing them at present." These "fits of spleen" were a well known trait in Townshend's personality. It made him "impatient of contradiction...impetuous and overbearing". His language was rough and inelegant and he was often "perplexed in argument". With all these shortcomings it may seem strange that he was chosen for this delicate diplomatic task. His main quality, somewhat unusual for his time, was his total honesty and integrity. He always made sure he had a thorough knowledge of the subject under discussion and so could make sensible contributions to it.

The failure of the negotiations was due as much to the prevarications of Townshend as the intransigence of the French. His method of negotiation was painfully slow and many of his schemes were impractical. His delays were partly the fault of the uncertainty at home and the lack of clear instructions. As the talks went on with no sign of progress, opinion in England became impatient. With the prospect of never-ending war the Whigs and Marlborough were further accused of continuing the war for their own ends. Horace Walpole wrote to his brother, "I am so far convinced that our divisions at home affect to the greatest degree, our negotiations, that I believe they are the reason why the French ministers will not speak to any purpose about peace and of late seem very haughty; and I don't doubt will continue so as long as the talk of a new ministry and new parliament is afoot." Finally, in June the first dismissal took place. Lord Sunderland, a member of the Whig "junta" and Secretary of State was removed from office. To prevent a collapse of confidence in the government, the Queen maintained that there would be no further changes although she refused to guarantee that Parliament would not be dismissed. In August, however, Lord Godolphin, the Lord Treasurer, was replaced by a Tory and negotiations in Holland became almost impossible. Finally, in May 1711, Townshend abandoned the effort and resigned.

Thus ended Townshend's first period in government. He had held key positions at critical times and attracted much criticism for his handling of events. He had a reputation for diplomacy and the understanding and handling of foreign affairs which was greatly hampered by the uncertain political situation at home. Marlborough thought that although Townshend was an honest man, he did not understand the temper of the Dutch and he disassociated himself from the final Barrier Treaty. The triumph of the Tories in 1710 supporting a policy for a speedy end of the war meant the fall from power of both Townshend and Walpole. This political tragedy was accompanied by personal ones. In June 1709, his brother, Roger, had died "who although long ill, his death seems very sudden...I fear Bristol waters hastened his end." Between April and June 1711 his new-born daughter, wife and eldest son died, a reminder of the uncertainty of life in early eighteenth century England. It is to this very uncertainty that Townshend and Walpole owed their rise to power later in their careers.

Return to Power

Between 1710 and 1715, Townshend was out of office, and so we would expect him to have spent more time on his estates. His financial affairs were still being run efficiently by his ex-guardian, LeStrange, but in 1713 the task was hampered by the fact that Samuel Smith, the bailiff, had just died and previous to that, "the books had not been kept in a regular form for several years." Mr Smith was replaced by the Reverend Priestland who was to run the estate, sending regular letters and reports when Townshend was away in London for many years to come. In February 1713 he wrote describing a violent tempest which had taken the tiles off a barn at Coxford Abbey and blown down several cart lodges, although there had been little damage to most of the barns; "Fletcher's clay barn" at Rudham was an exception; it was "quite ruined" and many of the windows in the Hall had been shattered. He then gave details of all that was happening on the estate; activities that must have seemed so alien to Townshend in London. Marling, or the spreading of chalk-rich clay subsoils on the light lands, was considered essential to the improved agriculture of which Townshend was an advocate, but Priestland reported that little had been carried out; "rain and snow have made it very unfit for carting" so a new pit had been opened up on the "grass beck" where "the weather cannot hinder us until we sink deep." In March he wrote giving welcome news, "I hope, corn bearing this year (1713) so good a price, few tenants will be in arrears."

Michaelmas was the time of year when tenancies changed hands and Priestland knew what to look for in a suitable applicant. "I doubt not that your lordship will have a very good tenant. He (Mr Case) puts his son in who has married a young woman with £12000 to her fortune." However, even in the running of estate affairs, political considerations were important. In the days when only 40 shilling freeholders could vote in the countryside and ballots were not secret, it was important to treat the local freeholders well. A tenant in Stibbard "puts in for the next fell of Stibbard wood. He begs this as a favour and if granted, is willing to hold his farm for what term you please. He pays his rent very well; my only objection is that Mr Black will be very concerned at it as he is a freeholder and has three sons freeholders. Their interests will be lost and to one who knows the trouble and fatigue of an election, this is some argument..." There were at least 85 tenants on the estate when Priestland took over, many of whom were in arrears. LeStrange reported however that when the bills of taxes and repairs which had been paid by the tenants and not yet accounted for, were included in the accounts, the arrears would in fact be greatly reduced.

It was during this time out of office, in the year when the Treaty of Utrecht, which Townshend had spent so much time negotiating, was finally ratified by his Tory opponents, that Townshend remarried. This time it was not a marriage designed to further his political career as his first had been, but instead he chose his childhood friend and companion, Dorothy Walpole. In the years that followed the marriage, the friendship between Charles Townshend and Robert Walpole was at its strongest. Dorothy loved and admired her brother and it was the combination of Townshend's and Walpole's interests, Townshend in foreign affairs and Walpole in domestic policy, that made them such a formidable team.

A group portrait of the children by his second marriage of Charles Townshend, by Charles Jervas, painted in the early 1720s. The boys are George, Augustus, Horatio and Edward and the girls Dorothy and Mary. It is thought that the girl on the left of the picture is Henrietta, who married William, the third son of the first marriage (Copyright Christies)

Queen Anne died on August 1st 1714, precipitating the constitutional crisis that the Act of Settlement of 1701 had been designed to counteract. The crown was not to go to its rightful hereditary claimant, the Catholic son of James II, now living in exile in Lorraine, but to Anne's Protestant cousin, George Lewis, Elector of Hanover. The terms of the Act of Settlement were well known and immediately on Anne's death, George was declared king. The Tories who had come to power in 1710 were suspected of supporting the claims of James, and St John Viscount Bolingbroke, Anne's leading minister in her last years, had been fighting hard to keep open the option of recognising James as king. The Tories were unlikely to be popular with George, as they had taken Britain out of the European war in which Hanover was involved by signing the Treaty of Utrecht, and so their only vain hope of keeping power was to promote and secure the Stuart succession.

On the day of Queen Anne's death, the leading Tories met to consider their next move. The Bishop of Rochester, Francis Atterbury, wanted an immediate declaration of James III as the new king, whilst Bolingbroke counselled caution, and the dangerous seven weeks between the death of Queen Anne and the arrival of George I passed without incident. It was this lack of unity, resulting in continual hesitancy, which meant that the Jacobite cause was doomed to failure from the beginning.

It was to the Whigs and those Tories who had not supported the hated Treaty of Utrecht that George turned when he made his nominations to the Council of Regency for those to be in charge of the government until he could reach England. George's principal German adviser, Bothmar, had been in England since June in order to prepare the way for his king and quickly acquired the support of the Whigs. He acted as a go-between with English politicians and advised the king on ministerial appointments. He was obviously a man whose friendship was worth cultivating and the result was a complete change of cabinet for the first time in British history. Townshend, "bluff and boisterous as ever", found himself back in the centre of the struggle for political power in one of the most powerful positions in government as Secretary of State for the North, with Horace Walpole, Robert's brother, as his under secretary. He was responsible, not only for affairs at home, but also, as indicated by his title, in northern Europe, the area in which the

Portrait of James, first earl Stanhope by Sir Godfrey Kneller between 1705-10 (National Portrait Gallery, London.)

new king was particularly interested. The other secretary of state was General James Stanhope, while Robert Walpole too gained a lucrative position as Paymaster General. This post allowed its holder great scope for financial manipulation as he was free to invest the funds in his charge for his own gain until they had to be paid out. Although not a cabinet position, Walpole, through his friendship with Townshend, could make his views heard, and so the Norfolk influence over national affairs was great.

The first problem for the new government was the Jacobites and, as Secretary of State for the North, Townshend was deeply involved. The Jacobite cause had split the Tory party, and after Bolingbroke openly declared his support for James Stuart by fleeing to France to join him, the party was tainted with treason. Fear of a rebellion in favour of James Stuart was intense, and the atmosphere of unrest increased particularly after the flight of Bolingbroke. All Tories were suspect, a phobia that was no doubt encouraged by the Whigs for their own political ends. On the 20th October, the day of George I's coronation, there were demonstrations in Birmingham, Bristol, Nottingham and Derby. The election of the following February was also marred by continuing mob violence. The Townshend papers give a vivid insight into the mood of the government, often bordering on panic during these disturbed times which remind us how fragile was the political stability of these years.

The first move of the Cabinet was to put troops and Lord

Lieutenants on alert. As most of the support for the Stuarts was likely to be in Scotland, four regiments were sent north in March 1715, to join the three that were already there. There was much discussion in May as to whether ships committed to protecting shipping in the Baltic should in fact return to the Channel, ready to intercept James if he attempted to cross from France. There was a general feeling of unease within the country and in late May there were riots in London to coincide with the king's birthday. The Lord Mayor was sent to examine the prisoners taken after the riots in case any of them could be accused of treason. It was felt that a few executions would be a deterrent to others. There was also to be a purging of the army. "A stout enquiry should be made into the disposition of the officers of the army and any disaffected to the government be immediately removed." Riots and unrest continued through the summer, particularly in Staffordshire, Shropshire and Worcestershire. A cabinet colleague and future Secretary of State, Lord Cartaret, writing from the west Country, had heard rumours that the Cornish tinners had rebelled and that people there were generally discontented with the government. In June the first sentences were passed. Lord Townshend no doubt received many letters similar to one that survives, asking him to intercede in the cases of three gentlemen under prosecution after riots in Shrewsbury. Cases of 11 accused were discussed on June 14th by the cabinet and sentences agreed, although only after much discussion. Townshend's notes of the meeting contain many alterations and crossings out. Robert Andrews, for instance, was first to be pardoned, but this is crossed out and he was transported instead. Of the 11, five were to be executed, five transported and only one was pardoned. On July 21st Habeus Corpus was suspended, allowing persons to be detained on suspicion of treason. In July the Duke of Ormonde, the Tory-appointed chief of the army, fled to join Bolingbroke with James in France, and on August 1st Townshend ordered his horses and equipage to be seized and a warrant for this purpose was sent to his house in St James' Square. Unrest continued in the capital. For instance, on October 10th waggons were searched for arms, and Mr Dyer the notorious Tory pamphleteer taken into custody at the Elephant and Castle.

Oxford University was a particular hotbed of sedition, and on September 2nd Henry Hookeath, Mr Castleman of Balliol

45

College, Mr Cresswick of Worcester College and Mr Chester of Oriel College were taken into custody. The king was not impressed by a loyal address from the university and instead retorted "that as they had shown a manifest disrespect to his majesty's person and government in all their late proceedings, so His Majesty expected they should convince him of their loyalty by their actions and not by words."

Although the most immediate danger was in London and the English shires, the insurrection was likely to gain the most sustained support in Scotland where there was still much discontent with the Act of Union. On July 15th news came to Townshend that Jacobite forces with four or five hundred horse were gathering near Blairgowry, and there were fears for the safety of Perth. It was also thought likely that James would try and land on the south coast, and in August the Lord Lieutenants of Scotland as well as Hampshire, Somerset, Devon and Cornwall were sent to their counties. Writs were issued for the arrest of Lord Mar and Colonel George Hamilton, but both of these men were already in Scotland and had managed to rally 18 Scottish lords, bringing with them some 5,000 men. By August 24th soldiers were being embarked for Scotland, and on August 27th officers were ordered to return to their regiments if they were stationed in Scotland or Ireland. On the 6th September John, Earl of Mar, raised the Pretender's standard at Perth, but in the event, risings were localised and sporadic with support mainly coming from the Catholics rather than the lowland Presbyterian Scots. A group led by Thomas Forster of Northumberland reached Preston where they were intercepted by General Wills and surrendered in November. The only remaining rebels were now in Scotland, and in December James Stuart himself landed at Peterhead. In January he reached Perth and was about to take the bold step of being crowned king of Scotland. Townshend felt he would not have been so daring unless he was expecting help from France and that the only way to prevent this was a strong alliance with Austria and the United Provinces (Holland) which would convince France that support of James would mean war in Europe. By this time the Earl of Mar's troops were deserting and the government troops had been reinforced and joined by Dutch soldiers, supplied under the terms of the new Barrier Treaty with the United Provinces for the protection of the Protestant succession. James soon realised the hopelessness of his cause and embarked for France in February. All that now remained for Townshend to do was to punish enough rebels to serve as a severe example to others, and return the country to a peacetime footing, ensuring in the process that the Tories were thoroughly discredited and the Whigs firmly in power. 26 captured officers were executed and 700 of the rank and file were transported.

In May 1716 the Dutch soldiers were sent back and the sheriffs of Staffordshire and Newcastle were written to and complimented on their services to the king. By July the situation was quiet and Townshend felt secure enough to pardon many of the prisoners still held. That this crisis was handled so firmly and efficiently was largely the result of Townshend's clear thinking and hard work. The government had been thoroughly frightened by the Jacobite threat and unrest throughout Britain had shown that George I was not a universally popular choice for king. However, so long as James refused to give up his Catholicism, there really was little chance for his cause.

There was little about George I to endear him to his British subjects. He was far more interested in European affairs; although he had not become the direct successor to Anne until the death of his mother, Sophia, in 1713, he had known for 13 years that he would eventually inherit the British throne, but never managed to speak fluent English. He saw his new kingdom merely as a means of exerting more pressure on European politics, and ministers seeking royal favour were well advised to support the king, even when his foreign policy seemed to contradict that traditionally followed by Britain.

Townshend probably understood the workings of British foreign policy better than anyone else in 1715-16, and to begin with he was trusted by George. He was responsible for several significant treaties. His first concern was a strong alliance against France to deter her from supporting the Jacobites. Firstly a new barrier treaty was negotiated with the Dutch. Townshend sympathised with their fear of Austria, who had become their powerful neighbour as overlord of the Netherlands (now Belgium) in place of Spain. The Dutch would not allow Austrian troops into the Netherlands until Austria had handed over some strategically placed fortresses. These were to be garrisoned by Dutch troops who were to be paid by the Austrians. Not so popular with the British was Holland's demand for trading concessions which would give the Dutch exclusive rights of trade with the Netherlands, and the Austrians refused to accept any of these terms. Much of the work of negotiating with the Dutch was done not by Townshend, who could not leave England during the crisis of the Jacobite risings, but by his secretary, Horace Walpole, at the Hague, and work on the treaty was finally completed by the end of 1715.

In 1716 a treaty was signed with Austria as were new commercial agreements with Spain. It would seem, therefore, that British interests were now safeguarded by alliances with her traditional allies, leaving her long-standing enemy, France, isolated. This, however, did not suit the interests of George I, and it was the question of how far Hanoverian interests should be allowed to dominate British foreign policy that finally split the Whigs.

George I's interests were centred on the complex politics of the Baltic states. The return of Charles XII to Sweden brought about the reopening of the Northern War, with Denmark, Poland and Russia against Sweden. Hanover supported the allies and she claimed the former Swedish territories of Bremen and Verdun. Denmark, which had annexed them in 1712, was prepared to recognise this claim if George would then bring in the British navy to help gain supremacy at sea over Sweden, on condition that war was declared by October 1715. This involvement of the British navy was not popular in Britain, and Townshend felt the sending of ships to the Baltic left Britain vulnerable to Jacobite attack. Finally a small fleet under Sir John Norris, large enough to protect British merchant shipping in the area, was sent.

In the summer of 1716, with these disagreements over foreign policy still not settled, George, with Townshend's fellow Secretary of State, Stanhope, set off for Hanover. This visit was greatly against the advice of Townshend and the government. Townshend wrote to George's German advisor, Berndorf, in no uncertain terms. "We are all unanimously of opinion that His Majesty's absence from his British domains might prove of the utmost prejudice to his interests." They felt that the danger of rebellion at home was far from over. "The rage and spirit of that party is still far from being subdued." Townshend was afraid that the French might well take advantage of the king's absence to support a Jacobite rising. There were still foreign alliances to be finalised and the problems of communications between Hanover and London greatly hampered negotiations. Similarly, there were the problems of instructing the Baltic fleet from Hanover, but necessarily through London.

George was unmoved by this long and carefully reasoned letter and was determined to go. The next problem was how much power should be vested in his eldest son as regent while he was away. Townshend and his colleagues felt that unless the Prince of Wales had full powers as regent, the government could not be strong enough, and eventually the king reluctantly agreed to this.

Meanwhile the situation in France had changed radically with the death of Louis XIV and the succession of his infant son, which was accompanied by rivalry between prospective regents, the Duke of Orleans and Philip V of Spain, who also disagreed on the succession should the child-king die. In the event the Duke of Orleans became regent, but Philip V of Spain hoped for some influence, and this rivalry successsfuly divided France from Spain and made France willing to make an alliance with her former enemy, Britain. Such a strong European alliance suited George very well, but Townshend and the government in Britain wanted to be more cautious. They did not want to sign any treaty which was not also supported and signed by the Dutch. Horace Walpole in Holland made this point to the "States" (government) of Holland and the Pensionary (its leader) to allay fears that Britain would desert her support for the Barrier Treaty. Stanhope, however, eager to curry favour with George, worked hard on the continent to put together a treaty with France. This would include the expulsion of James Stuart to Italy. James now had to look for another sponsor and the most likely source of help seemed to be Britain's new enemy, Sweden. Sweden had traditionally been an ally of Britain's and Townshend saw the Northern War as being contrary to British interests. James and the Swedish government were certainly intriguing against Britain, and Townshend urged the king to make peace with Sweden as quickly as possible.

The letters which passed between Stanhope and Townshend in the autumn of 1716 show how completely the two secretaries of state were now at loggerheads. Stanhope wanted a final signing of the treaty with France as soon as possible, without waiting for the Dutch. He wanted the British fleet to stay in the Baltic through the winter because there was fear that Russia was intending to invade Denmark, whilst Townshend could see no wisdom in this and wanted the war speedily concluded.

His characteristic bad temper and impatience shows through the normally formal language of his letters. "This northern war has been managed so stupidly that it will be our ruin." (letter to Stanhope in October 1716) Later Townshend's secretary, Stephen Pointz, wrote, "He (Townshend) commands me to acquaint you that it makes him loose all patience to see what ridiculous expedients they propose to His Majesty for extricating themselves out of their present difficulties; as if the leaving of 8 men-of-war to be frozen up for 6 months would signify 5 grains towards giving a new turn to affairs in the north."

Much of Townshend's argument against Stanhope and the king's northern policy was carefully reasoned; for instance, his arguments for the return of Sir John Norris and his fleet before the winter seem eminently sensible. "It will above all things be necessary for His Majesty's service, that Sir John Norris should be at liberty to return with the fleet by the beginning of November at the farthest, not only on account of the danger to which merchantmen would be exposed without his convoy (which yet in our present circumstances is alone sufficient to make his stay impracticable) but because our sea officers are all of opinion that the ships which winter there will certainly be so far damaged by the frosts (which begin usually in November) and by other accidents in those seas that they will scarce be fit for any other expedition. Besides they cannot be of any use or service there during the winter season and our officers are all clear in their opinion, that the squadron may return thither earlier in the next spring from England, than they can be fitted for action in those parts after the thaw." Neither did Townshend want to get involved in a war against Russia, an important trading partner and most importantly a supplier of naval stores. George was particularly annoyed, because in all this Townshend seemed to be getting the support of the Prince of Wales, thus increasing the rift between father and son that had already existed.

Meanwhile plans for the French treaty were progressing too fast for Townshend's liking and Horace Walpole was finding his position at the Hague more and more embarassing. On October 16th Stanhope sent instructions that the French treaty should now be signed, in spite of the fact that the Dutch were not ready. Walpole immediately requested that he be allowed to return to

England on the grounds of ill health "in case we be obliged to sign before the States are ready, which for my part, I never can in honour or conscience do, though I should have been extremely proud to have put the last hand to this treaty could it have been done upon a right foot." Townshend did not want to see Walpole return and hoped instead to be able to delay the preparation of the document giving him the full powers that he needed to sign, which would allow the final negotiations with the Dutch to take place. These negotiations were necessarily long winded because of the highly complicated Dutch constitution. The seven provinces did not form one republic, but a confederation, and each province was itself a confederacy of the constituent cities and towns who sent deputies to the provincial "state" or council. Before any treaty could be ratified, it had to be agreed by all the separate provinces and it was this that was taking the time.

Finally Walpole managed to gain the necessary permission to return to England, thus avoiding the need to sign the treaty before the Dutch, and was immediatly sent on a mission to Hanover to try and explain the government's position to the king. Townshend was feeling very frustrated by the lack of cooperation being shown by his colleague and fellow Secretary of State, Stanhope, who was in Hanover, and on October 16th 1716 he wrote to him, "I can struggle no longer against the difficulties which our enemies about the king create us every day, and shall therefore most earnestly beg leave to resign my employment and to retire into the country as soon as the king returns." Townshend blamed the "malicious insinuations" that were being made to the king about Walpole and himself on the kings German adviser, Bothmar. Little did he realise that the greatest of his enemies at this time was Stanhope himself, determined, along with Sunderland who had joined him in Hanover, to oust Townshend and Walpole from office. However, the time was not yet ripe for Stanhope who swiftly replied to Townshend's letter, "if you knew how thoroughly well the king thinks of your lordship, and how often he upon all occasions express it, I am sure you would not have (suggested resigning) said it yourself".

By November things had changed. The king was displeased over the delays put in the way of signing the French treaty and felt that rather than being loyal ministers, Townshend and Walpole were hand-in-glove with the wayward Prince of Wales and his party. On December 15th Townshend was demoted to Lord Lieutenant of Ireland. Townshend reacted to this snub by writing a long letter to the king defending his actions and roundly denying the king's accusations. While there was some truth in the charge that Townshend had been deliberately slowing down the process of signing the French treaty, there is no evidence that he was in league with the prince against his father, although certainly and of necessity they had a close working relationship during the king's absence in Hanover. Townshend had no wish to go to Ireland and refused the post on the grounds that "domestic affairs do not permit me to reside outside England." Instead he asked permission "to attend to the private affairs of my family which I have long neglected." He was persuaded to accept the post, although he never visited Ireland, only holding it for a few months before he was finally sacked.

The final break came over the clash between British and Hanoverian interests. Stanhope was willing to support George while Townshend was not. "Stanhope owed his ascendancy to loyalty to the Elector of Hanover rather than the king of Great Britain." On April 17th details of a Jacobite plot involving the Swedish ambassador in London, Count Gyllenborg, were laid before parliament. The seriousness of the plot was stressed in an effort to persuade parliament to declare war on Sweden. When the issue was put to the House of Commons, Walpole refused to support it and the government majority fell to four. On the same day Townshend was dismissed and the next day Walpole and most of his supporters resigned, leaving Stanhope in power. Townshend had learnt his lesson. Never again when he was in office would he allow a political rival to accompany the king to Hanover. He would make sure that he was always there. Meanwhile it was a question of biding his time, and he returned to his Norfolk estates for the first time in two and a half years.

Townshend's work as Secretary of State had not only involved him in affairs of the highest national and international importance, but also in dealing with a wide-ranging post-bag of requests and begging letters. All demanded attention because causing offence could lose his party and particularly his relatives in the House of Commons, electoral support. Some of the petitions involved trade. His papers for 1715 and 1716 include a petition from merchants of Waterford for a naval escort to take 100 tons of butter to Constantinople, the Turks having lost their regular supply from Russia because of the Northern War. They pointed out the profits that there would be for the Crown in excise if the expedition was successful. A second petition was from English merchants in Algiers whose ship, seized by the Algerians and then sold to the English was now being held by the Dutch. The English merchants wanted help in getting it back.

By far the most common type of petition was for support in getting a position in the army, government or the church. Help was asked in "obtaining the place of master carpenter of his majesty's works, vacant by the death of Mr J Churchill." Similarly, "Mr Trebick is now extreemely ill, and in all probability cannot live two days longer: and in case of his death there will be a place of Gentleman of his Majesty's Chapel Royal vacant, in which I should be very glad to succeed him." Making a start in the world involved the writing of endless letters to those with influence in the hope that eventually a post, however junior, would be granted. "James Fraser of Foyes is a gentleman about 30 years old, a relation of my Lord Lovat's and has a vote in the shire of Inverness...His family has suffered very much by the great expense that his father and brother were at against the rebels in 1715 and they having died, and leaving this young man in great trouble and for the debts they had contracted serving the king during the great rebellion, for which they never had the least reward. My Lord Lovat humbly entreats that the said James Fraser may be made a subaltern officer of his independent company since he will answer for his fidelity and good behaviour."

Nowhere is there any indication as to whether these petitioners were successful, or whether instead they took their cause on elsewhere in their search for a breakthrough into their chosen profession.

Although embittered by the treachery of his colleague in office, Stanhope, it must have been with some relief that Townshend left both the great affairs of state and the constant bombardment of petty personal petitions behind him and travelled to his Norfolk estates in the spring of 1716. Already in his 40s and only too well aware, from family bereavement, of the uncertainty of life in an age of sudden and violent illness, Townshend may well have wondered whether his political career was at an end, rather than simply suffering a temporary setback.

The Years of Achievement

Between 1717 and 1719 Townshend and Walpole were in opposition, which may have allowed Townshend to spend more time at Raynham. Although there are no surviving London account books between 1717 and 1720, Townshend did still spend some time there. He joined the Tories in the House of Lords in supporting the Earl of Oxford who had been impeached by the Whigs for his part in securing the Tory-inspired Treaty of Utrecht. If the Earl had been found guilty he would not only have been disgraced but could also have been imprisoned. Townshend argued against his own party to secure the Earl of Oxford's freedom. Walpole also exercised great influence in the House of Commons, and his constant attendance would have been needed to keep his followers united and continually opposing the government. By 1720 Walpole's tactics were paying off, and Sunderland, now first Lord of the Treasury, finding he needed the support of Walpole's group, appointed Townshend to the position of President of the Council and Walpole to the lucrative post of Paymaster to the Forces.

The fall of Sunderland's government became inevitable with the of the South Sea Company, resulting in a general loss of confidence in the financial markets and the implication of both the government and the royal family in fraudulent activities aimed at inflating the value of South Sea shares. Although Sunderland was declared innocent of deception, his government could not survive, and Walpole became first Lord of the Treasury. With the death of Lord Stanhope, Townshend returned to his old post of Secretary of State for the North alongside Carteret who was Secretary for the South.

In spite of their disagreements in the past, Townshend wrote on hearing of the death of Stanhope, that he had lost "a kind and sincere friend." The Secretary of State for the South, John Cartaret, regarded Townshend as a dangerous rival and was intent on increasing his influence at Townshend's expense.

One of Townshend's first concerns as Secretary was to help his Norfolk supporters. Although he himself sat in the House of Lords, the power of his party was firmly rooted in the House of Commons, and so the complaints of the Norfolk and Norwich voters had to be heard. The wealth of the city of Norwich was based on the weaving of woollen and, more recently, silk textiles. In 1720 through Lord Townshend, the "Mayor, Sheriff, citizens and commonality of the City of Norwich" petitioned the House of Lords for help to reverse the depression in the textile industry of Norwich resulting from the imports of Indian calicoes. The city wanted the Lords to support a bill prohibiting the use and wearing of calicoes, and later in the year such a bill did in fact become law.

On their return to power, Townshend and Walpole found that the Jacobite threat was as pressing as ever. After the suppression of the rebels in 1716, Townshend had written, "The rage and spirit of the party is far from being subdued...the fire of the rebellion is rather smothered for a time than totally extinguished." Stanhope and Sunderland had kept up the vigilance and a great anti-Jacobite spy network was operating throughout Britain and Europe. The South Sea Bubble crisis provided the ideal opportunity for the Jacobites to catch the government unprepared. The trouble was that they still lacked the backing of a major foreign power and were so torn by indecision that they did little in the months of greatest government crisis between September and December 1720. Francis Atterbury had been one who had always wanted independent action, and he wrote to James, "The time is now come, when with very little assistance from your friends abroad, your way to your friends at home is become safe and easy." Finally, by late 1721, a plan for a rebellion, relying on very little foreign help, was put together.

Of great importance in the organisation of this plot was the Norfolk lawyer from Aylsham, Christopher Layer. He crossed to the Continent several times to meet James and showed him a list of Norfolk gentry and others, with an estimate of their wealth, who were prepared to support the Stuart cause. Many of the people on this list look very unlikely supporters of such an adventure, and it is more a list of Tory sympathisers than of Jacobites. The plans were drawn up and blank receipts, signed by James, were issued to sympathisers for the buying of provisions and arms. The rising was to be during the election of 1722, but after their initial enthusiasm, many began to lose heart and felt that the money would be better spent influencing the election rather than buying arms.

From the beginning, the plans of the plotters had been intercepted and their coded letters deciphered. Some of these letters survive at Raynham. There were two main types of code, one which relied on numbers representing words, names or letters and another where words and phrases took on new meanings. All the main leaders had code or "cant" names, often beginning with the correct initial. For instance, Mrs Jane was James, Mr Manson was the Earl of Mar, and Harriot, the Duke of Hamilton. Other frequently used cyphered words and phrases were "law suit" for "Pretender's cause", "commerce" for "conspiracy", "carpenters" for "Scottish soldiers", "sadlers" for "Irish soldiers", and "creditors" for "ministers".

In April 1722, the arrests "and one of the greatest witch hunts in British history" began. There was a clampdown on communication with France, the Tower of London was garrisoned and spy activity increased. On 8th May, Townshend saw the Lord Mayor of London and disclosed to him what information he had on the plot, and the anti-Catholic laws were brought into operation. On 10th May the governor of Edinburgh castle and other Scottish garrisons were put on alert.

It was not until 24th August that enough evidence was gathered together to allow for the arrest of Atterbury, and Layer was arrested on 1st September. When his rooms were searched, detailed plans for the insurrection, plus a bundle of blank receipts signed by James were found. On 9th October, Habeus Corpus was suspended allowing the Government to keep its many suspects in custody, and a very detailed enquiry by a Committee of Council began. Its meticulous work was closely watched by both Walpole and Townshend, but it could only produce enough firm evidence to allow for the trial and execution of Layer. He was brought to trial on November 21st, but his execution was delayed until the following May in the hope that more evidence could be extracted from him. The evidence against Atterbury was still lacking. "Though his sympathy for the cause was notorious, the evidence for his share in the Jacobite plot was weak." Townshend and Walpole had to content themselves with his banishment, and on the 18th June he left. The government knew that as long as Atterbury was alive, and he lived until 1732, there was a very real danger of a Jacobite rebellion.

Townshend's main interest was, as always, foreign policy, and one of his first actions on returning to power was to break with the traditional Whig anti-French policies of 1709–10 and 1714–15 and to write to the French regent stating his firm intention of remaining on friendly terms with France; a policy that was essential if Britain was to be sure that the Pretender was to receive no support from there. Cartaret was not prepared to accept the seniority of Townshend. His supporter, Sir Luke Schaub, was the British ambassador in Paris, and through him Cartaret was planning to strengthen his influence there. To undermine Schaub's position, Robert's brother, Horace Walpole, was sent to the French court as an unofficial rival ambassador and he soon gained the ear of members of the regency council and so weakened Cartaret's position.

If the Pretender could expect no support from France, then he had to turn to Austria, Spain and Russia, and it was in these courts that Townshend was on the lookout for plots. An agent in the Hague reported in April 1722, that "The partisans of Austria here are of late very industrious to divulge with a great deal of affectation, that there is some design on foot between the king of Spain and the regent of France on behalf of the Pretender, and that all the levies made in these parts for Spain are to be employed for the service of the last." The rumours were still rife in September and when an envoy, Sir Anthony Westcombe, returned from Spain and arrived at Falmouth, he wrote to Townshend that he would speak to no one else until he had given his information to the Secretary of State.

In 1723 both Carteret and Townshend went with George I to Hanover. Townshend had learnt the danger of allowing others to influence the king in his absence, and so, in spite of the cost (£4500 in 1723) and the inconvenience of moving his family and being away from Raynham, Townshend made the journey. Townshend managed to gain the upper hand, and Schaub was recalled to be replaced at the French court by Horace Walpole.

For George, British concerns were always secondary to those of Hanover, and once there, the threat of a Russian invasion of Sweden became his main worry. Rumours were rife and the Russian navy was said to have been sighted on several occasions. Townshend wrote to Walpole in July asking that £2000 be put in readiness for the support of Sweden if the need arose. In this lay one of the reasons for the conflict which later arose between Townshend and Walpole. Walpole's main aim was to restore confidence in the British money markets, shattered by the South Sea Bubble scandal, by keeping peace, thus enabling the reduction of taxes. Townshend was more concerned with the defence of British and sometimes Hanoverian interests. Whilst there was the fear of a Jacobite rebellion supported by a European ally, the supporting of these interests would be expensive, and a disaffected Sweden was a very likely source of support for exiled James.

Although Walpole agreed to make the money available to Townshend, he wrote, "In a word, *my politics are to keep free from all engagements as long as we possibly can. You'll forgive my sudden and possibly very improper thoughts upon a subject that I am but little acquainted with, but I am mightily inclined to be cautious...*In short I wish to God we may at least for a little time remain neutral and look on, if all the rest of Europe does the same thing. But all this I submit to your better judgement."

The other thing that was worrying Walpole were the reports of a split between Carteret and Townshend that were reaching London. The fear that there might be changes at the top of the government was unsettling and did not help Walpole in his main aim of creating stability both in the financial world and in the country as a whole. Townshend, however, was confident that his views were finding favour with the king and that gradually he was gaining the upper hand. To prove this, he wrote to Walpole, "The king continues in his resolution of signing no paper relating to his British affairs, except in my presence." In his efforts to gain royal favour, Carteret had allied himself with the king's German adviser, Bernstorf, who wanted ships sent to the Baltic to thwart the Russian invasion, but Townshend, well aware of Walpole's views on the subject and the difficulty of getting such a request through parliament, did not.

Although he was a diplomat, Townshend was an honest man who believed in straight dealing and he found the court of Hanover a wearing place in which to operate. "If there be a place in the world where faction and intrigue are natural and in fashion, it is here, which makes it no easy task for a stranger to behave himself inoffensively; however, I am very sure I have lost no friend, and I think I have made no enemy; tho' it is not a very agreeable situation to be eternally upon one's guard from all quarters." He was, however, able to intrigue with the best of them and gain the ear of George I's mistress, the Duchess of Kendal. He was correct in thinking he was gaining influence with the king, who finally, as August arrived and the threat of the Russian invasion of Sweden declined, came to agree with Townshend over the wisdom of holding back from sending a fleet to the Baltic. In early December, with the king and his court back from Hanover, Carteret's position was becoming weaker and he was finally dismissed as Secretary of State and replaced by Thomas Pelham Holles, Duke of Newcastle. A man renowned for his generosity and extravagance, he was the brother of Townshend's first wife and the two men were close friends. His almost childish need for affection led him to make promises he could not fulfil and so to accusations of untruthfulness and double dealing. He was constantly busy in political and public affairs and like Townshend, he could be short tempered. His many limitations and lack of judgement meant that there was never any doubt that Townshend would be the senior partner.

The years 1724-5 saw Townshend and Walpole at the height of their power. Their popularity was helped by a period of peace abroad and prosperity at home. The king remained in England in 1724, adding to the general sense of security and well being. The team of Townshend and Walpole was working well, partly because of the influence of Walpole's sister, Lady Townshend. Townshend remained popular and influential with the king, and perhaps more importantly his mistress, the Duchess of Kendal. The degree of this power is illustrated in the following extract from a letter of the French Ambassador, Count Broglio, to the king of France: "Lord Townshend and Mr Walpole have lately been indisposed, but they are now quite recovered. It is much to be wished, that they should remain in power, for they appear anxious to maintain the good intelligence which subsists between the two (British and French) crowns; they possess an unbounded influence over the king and the Duchess of Kendal."

There is also the possibly apocryphal story of the granting of the Order of the Garter to Townshend. In an attempt to reconcile the Prince of Wales to his father, Townshend and Walpole promised that they would persuade the king to award the Earl of Scarborough, the prince's close friend and Master of his Horse, the Order of the Garter. When there were two vacant positions (the king always wanted to keep one free), Townshend requested the position for Scarborough. The king replied that he could not comply with the request as it was already given. Townshend was surprised and asked to whom, to which the king replied that it was for Townshend. Townshend declined, the king insisted, but

Townshend would not agree until the king offered the Order to both himself and Scarborough, thus forcing the king to break his usual rule of leaving one vacant. Influenced by Townshend, the king was persuaded to delay his departure for Hanover and it was not until June 1725 that, accompanied by Townshend, he finally set out again.

It was during this period, when Townshend's power was at its strongest, that he embarked on a major series of improvements at Raynham. Although some maintenance and renovation work had gone on almost continuously since Townshend came of age, it was not until the 1720s that he sought the advice of London's most fashionable designer, William Kent and then employed London craftsmen to carry out his plans.

In 1724, Townshend began work on the lake and removed most of the formal gardens around the house, opening up the wide views which were becoming an important element of park design. Alongside work in the park went work in the house. Although the work carried out was substantial, the basic layout of the earlier house remained. The former chapel was converted into a grand saloon and the marble entrance hall was remodelled to become "the show-piece of black-and-white classical elegance it is today." One wonders whether the many years spent by Townshend in Holland account for the very Dutch feel of this charming room which seems full of light on even the darkest day. Here as elsewhere the doorways and mouldings are designed by Kent and his chimney pieces remain throughout the house. By 1731, when most of the work was complete, Raynham would have been at the forefront of fashion and good taste, without the ostentation of the new houses being erected by his neighbours at Houghton and Holkham.

The period of calm and tranquility with Walpole and Townshend working in undisputed harmony was not to last. Two problems arose, one at home and one abroad. The situation in Scotland was a continual worry in both British and foreign affairs. Townshend was always concerned that foreign powers would be tempted into giving support to the Jacobite cause and there was always dissatisfaction in Scotland to give hope to James. A strike of brewers in Edinburgh over attempts to raise a malt duty led to a situation that Walpole feared "will come to a serious matter, and prove as difficult to tackle as anything that has happened since His Majesty's accession." As a result of prompt action by the Earl of

Islay, the trouble did not spread; but it did serve as a reminder of the dangerous situation north of the border and made Townshend all the more determined to link Britain in defensive alliances that would dissuade her enemies from supporting the Pretender.

Once back in Hanover, it was clear that the danger of a Russian invasion of Sweden was by no means over and further disagreements between Walpole and Townshend about how much money should be made available to support the Swedes took place. Walpole was adamant that no more than £50,000 should be drawn on the public revenue. There were further causes for disagreement as summer passed into autumn and the king and Townshend were still in Hanover. In September 1725 Townshend negotiated the Treaty of Hanover, a defensive alliance of England, France and Prussia. This was the first piece of Townshend's foreign policy which Walpole categorically opposed and he chose to take little part in the House of Commons debate considering the Treaty.

This alliance, far from securing the strong peace that Walpole desired, was seen as setting the stage for another European war with the signatories of the Treaty of Hanover ranged against Spain, Portugal, Austria and Russia (already linked by the Treaty of Vienna). Spain openly showed her support for the Pretender and was threatening Gibraltar. Austria prepared to help co-operate with Catherine of Russia in an invasion of Britain which was to be attempted at the same time from the coasts of Russia, Norway, Flanders and Spain. There were fears in July 1726 that a joint Spanish/Russian fleet was gathering in Spain, and in November the commander of Gibraltar was buying up coal in preparation for a siege. Although the danger of an immediate invasion passed, Townshend was still looking for ways to increase his allies. In August 1726 the Dutch signed the Treaty, and in 1727 Sweden and Denmark followed. Walpole, in contrast, was looking for an opportunity for reconciliation, if possible with both Austria and Spain, but failing that with one of them. For the first time these partners in government were pulling in opposite directions as far as foreign policy was concerned. Up to this time, Walpole had been prepared to leave foreign affairs to the well-travelled Townshend but after 1725-6, this changed. In 1727, just before the death of George I, the Preliminaries of Paris were signed which ended the threat of conflict. Austria agreed to suspend the activities of the Ostend Company, whose trading was a threat to Britain, and the chances of a period of prolonged peace looked good. Keeping up alliances in readiness for war always led to expense which Walpole wished to avoid, and there was bound to be a clash between Walpole's financial caution and Townshend's desire for security against Jacobite invasion supported by a foreign power.

Only Townshend remained cautious and wanted to remain ready for war. This was a difficult policy to persuade the House of Commons to accept and Townshend found himself at odds with the rest of the cabinet.

The strongest tie between the two men had been Townshend's second wife and Walpole's sister, Dorothy. She formed the link with the happy childhood they had all spent together and had great influence over both her husband and her brother, reducing the tension between them. In March 1726 she died of smallpox at the age of 40 and this mediating force was lost. She had been a loyal wife and had travelled abroad with her husband where she soon developed the "manners of court" and a natural ease of conversation with both British and foreign politicians and diplomats which ensured she would be sadly missed. With this loss of the personal bond between the two men, their relationship rapidly deteriorated.

While negotiations with Austria were going on, news of another possible Jacobite plot was being reported to Townshend. There was some evidence from intercepted letters that Austria, Spain and Russia were prepared to support the Pretender, but in spite of his obsession with Jacobitism, Walpole was not prepared to rush into the panic measures that Townshend recommended, such as intercepting Russian ships to search for arms on their way to the Jacobites. He thought that the king and Townshend were "too much alarmed with the exaggerated rumours and apprehensions of distant evil." Walpole believed that imminent invasion was the only excuse for war that either he or Parliament would accept. He regarded Austria as Britain's natural ally against an ambitious France and was afraid, rightly as it turned out, that France would not pay her share of the necessary subsidies, leaving Britain paying the full sum. More worrying was a "wild scheme" put to Horace Walpole in Paris by Townshend for invading the Austrian Netherlands and partitioning them between France and Holland. It was to ensure the continued alliance with France that Townshend had tried to persuade George to marry his daughter into the French rather than the Prussian royal family, but to George, his German interests were always paramount and in 1726 he had to write to Horace Walpole in Paris saying that he had failed.

Hardly a letter passed between the two ministers that did not point to the deepening rift between them over foreign policy; yet even at this stage of their disintegrating friendship, there was much that they still shared and valued. Walpole had been able to leave London for a few weeks and get back to their beloved Norfolk, and Townshend began his letter, "I am glad to hear you have had such good weather, so fine a season and so much diversion in Norfolk."

It was early in 1727, that a further Jacobite plot came to Townshend's notice. A merchant from Leith and a known Jacobite sympathiser, John Strachan, was brought to London and examined by Townshend in the Cabinet Council to explain letters addressed to him which had been intercepted when a trading vessel from Spain had been searched. Spies reported that Spain had "forty six good transport ships and the best sail in Europe ready for this design." 4,000 men were to be landed in Scotland and 8,000 in England while 400 broadswords "all designed for gentlemen" had been landed at Leith. A Captain Sinclair was searching the west coast of Scotland for a suitable landing place while a companion, Captain Brown, was active in England. Papers recently discovered at Raynham show that Rob Roy MacGregor of Balquidder was scouring the Highlands for information for the government. Known amongst the clans as a Jacobite who had led his MacGregor regiments under the Earl of Mar and played his part in the Spanish invasion fiasco of 1718 when troops, disembarked from Spanish ships, had been captured at Glensheil and a Jacobite rising foiled, he would have been able to gain local confidence easily. He may well have been disillusioned by the Jacobites' lack of ability to organise an invasion which was so obvious in 1718 and again in the failed attempt at a Spanish landing in 1719. Rob Roy could see that the cause was doomed to failure. Sir Walter Scott quotes a letter written in 1720 by Rob Roy to General Wade, who was at that time disarming the Highland clans and building military roads, in which he states that he had been forced into an "unnatural rebellion against King George", but that he had never acted "offensively against his majesty's forces" and had instead sent "what intelligence he could collect from time to time." Whatever was the truth, he seemed to have still been trusted by the Highland Jacobites and also to have been in communication with those in Spain. To prove his connections at the exiled Jacobite court in Spain, Rob Roy forwarded a letter to General Wade telling him of the arrival of Captain Sinclair and Captain Brown and the purpose of their visit. In return for his information, Rob Roy expected the government to pay his expenses travelling around the Highlands and a pension for life, "for I need not tell you my narrow circumstances occasioned by all the cross accidents and circumstances of my life...If I were encouraged to go in this affair, I'll engage under the penalty of losing my life to get full intelligence of all the plots and projects, they can contrive or imagine of landing in this nation, and likewise of any persons that will go into their measures." (letter from Rob Roy to Sir Duncan Campbell, February 1727 Raynham ms) Despite several arrests and questioning, this plot seems to have fizzled out like so many others, but it did emphasise to the government the need to establish friendly relations with all the powers from whom the Pretender could hope for support.

In June 1727 Townshend set out on his first foreign mission without his wife to join George I in Hanover. The king had set out before him and was on his way to see his brother, the Bishop of Osnabruck, when he was taken ill in his carriage and died of a stroke. Townshend, as soon as he heard the news, went straight to Osnabruck where the king's body had been taken. From there he wrote a letter of congratulation and condolence to the new king, George II, and returned to England.

The future for Townshend and Walpole was by no means secure. Although Walpole had organised a reconciliation between George I and his son, it had been very superficial, and George II still considered Walpole as one of his father's ministers, which would certainly go against him now. When Walpole told the new king of his father's death George made no pretence of sorrow, but instead asked Walpole to fetch his friend and Speaker of the Commons, Sir Spencer Compton, presumably with the intention of promoting him to high office. Compton however lacked political ability and even asked Walpole to write the Commons' loyal address to the new king. It was not difficult for Walpole to out-manoeuvre such a man. In particular, Walpole had courted the favour of Queen

Caroline and had been astute enough to realise that although the new king preferred the company of his mistress, he respected the views of the queen more, and by the end of 1727 he was firmly back in power. This gave Walpole the upper hand in the Walpole-Townshend partnership and left Townshend in a vulnerable position. On his return from Hanover Townshend was very ill. At 53, he had reached what was regarded as a good age in the eighteenth century, and he never really recovered his youthful vigour and stamina for political battle; it was this illness that Townshend gave to foreign diplomats as the reason for his resignation in 1730. At this stage Walpole's letters to Townshend made it clear that he still valued their friendship and there was certainly no suggestion that he wanted him to go.

Extracts (pp65–67) from one of the many documents showing the work of government spies in unearthing Jacobite plots. The letter, supposedly from the Pretender, shows the number code and how it has been translated by the code breaker (by kind permission, Lord Townshend)

The following is the full transcript of the letter dated December 11th 1726 from Killoch (the Pretender) to Mr Robert Burnett, including the decyphering.

Yours of the 9th Septemb. and 2d Octr came safe to me, as well as one of the 14th Sept. with a letter from Mr Cotton to whom You'll forward the Inclosed Answer. What I writ to you of the 13th Novemr about Mr

Manson (Earl of Mar) will sufficiently show you my Sentiments as to Him upon what You now write to me concerning Him, and that it is by no means fit that any who wish Mrs Jane (the king) well should have any dealings with Him in Relation to 2128381315 37251229 (publick) 243320283324372214203 (Affairs) Since he neither has, nor never will have any 14354292226, (share) 3723288 (in) 11422010 (my) 251733337192623312526 (confidence) and that His being able to 131724141829 (boast) 17333110 (of) 2428234228 (any) 2517222 8282226142 111723192623102526 (correspondence) with Mrs Jane's (the king) friends, only serves to give 3531371120 (him) 2522261 937182920, 4537183520, 1835171 42628 (credit with Those) whom he would 3711211714262029, 3821201726 (impose upon) by a shew of 402624152910, 3317220, 1142102831 (Zeal for my service) 1426224737252631. But if either Laurence or any Body else have private affairs which engage Them to 45222837182620 (write to him) 18281710, 3531171129, I shall have nothing to say against it, Since I don't enter into the private Concern of particular persons.

I am much concerned at Harriot's (The Duke of Hamilton's)
1524182610, 2517261938251828 (late conduct) for whatever Her
(his) private 372318372828172314 (Intentions) 1124421031, 132
639, 18352628, 2138131537251229, 2421292921262422242325
1026 (the Public Appearance) She (he) has made, must necessarily very
much diminish Her (his) 25222619371820, 372329, 3537142828,
202517382318222632, (credit in his country) and by consequence her
(his) 24133715371842142910, 182017, 142622472629, 28112628,
37231020, 31371829 (abilities to serve me in it) and in Her (his) present
Situation I think Thomson should equally avoid 18352631 37112124
22182837231420 (the imparting) 31181728, 3520371120 (to Him)
any 142625222826181429 17332810 371121172182423252628
(Secrets of Importance) or the shewing of 3520371120, 242028,
2226142622472629, 17223110, 2517313117152326143914 (Him a
Reserve or Coolness) which may 2115382314262028, 353711 (plunge
him) yet further into Her (his) present 2011262414382226141029
(measures) and make her (him) less inclined to 33242847172220,
28114210, 252924381426 (favouring my cause) on proper occasions.

I have nothing further to add at present in Answer to Your last
Letters, But as the Appearance of William (war) 19242842154228,
26232522312624142614, 1473910, 1917261428, 114229928, 351
721261429, 17332839 (daily encreases so does my Hopes of) being able
to 251729112610, 18281729, 421738221028, 241429391437141824
2322526. (come to Your assistance) The family is well and my constant
Kindness ever attends you.

Killoch (The Pretender)

N.B. The letter signed Killoch is plainly the Pretenders'

1) Because of the stile

2) Persons very well acquainted with his handwriting affarm that the
signature, Killoch, was written by the Pretender

3) It is remarkable that one of the Cypher-Keys seised on Lord Garlie
happens to have under the letter K, the word Killoch, to denote the King
i.e. the Pretender

All those parts of the letters that are marked underneath with red lines were
written in cyphers; and such of the cant-names as have words written over
them, are supposed to mean those words. It is likewise supposed that all
cant-words stand for words beginning with the same letter.

N.B.

The Letter signed Killoch is
plainly the Pretender's
1°. Because of the Stile.
2°. Persons very well acquainted
with his hand-writing affirm that the
Signature Killoch was written by the
Pretender.
3°. It is remarkable that one
of the Cypher-keys seised on Lord Garlie
happens to have, under the Letter K. the
word Killoch, to denote the King i.e. the
Pretender.

All those parts of the Letters
that are markt underneath with red Lines,
were written in Cyphers; and such of the
Cant-names as have words written over
them, are supposed to mean those words.
It is likewise supposed that all Cant-words
stand for Words beginning with the same
Letter.

Note referring to the letter on pp65–68; the transcript of which is given opposite.

Dec 11, 1726. Copy of a letter directed to Mr Robert Burnet, and signed Issabella (lord Inverness) Decyphered.

(Author's note: code numbers have not been included in the transcript but decoded words are in brackets)

I need not trouble you with a long letter in answer to yours of the 10th September, Since I think I can do it to your satisfaction in a very few words. I know nothing of any Lisles (letters) (from Mar to the Queen being intercepted) neither do I believe him so imprudent as to put (into writing) what you say 'tis pretended by some, he did, so I think I need say no more to you on that article.

I never had, Sir, any doubt of Freeman's (honesty) On the contrary, have of a long time a very great value for (him) And what was said either by Kennedy (the king) or me of particular (Persons) in the letters which you answer, was chiefly meand for (their) information, and as a friendly act. Since Mrs Jane (the king) was very apt to believe that perhaps more was bragg'd of than was real, which will likewise, I hope, explain to you what I said to Campden and the reason why I mentioned particularly (two noble lords) in relation to what was said to Conti, was because they had sent (memorials hither) on that subject, which if you don't know from themselves, You need to take no notice to had it from me. I am very much of opinion that frank and open dealling is the best, especially, when one is concerned in the affairs of others, and according to that maxim, and on accn't of the friendships I have for Laurence, I should certainly have mentioned to him any charge that might have been layed to his door, But I think without encroaching upon either, I would be wrong, If at any time, I amused Laurence with what is of (no consequence) and has (no weight), and plainly proceeds from humor, infirmities or the like, from which you'll observe that this part of my letter is designed for Laurence (alone.)

Assure Conti that I have (layd before the King their assurances of steadfast adherence to service, readyness to conform) to his (orders and direction in) all matters, In return to which Mrs Jane (the king orders me to inform them of) the satisfaction she (he) had in being informed of the good reception (they) gave to her (his) late endeavors for the wellfare of Chichelle, which she (he) desires Conti may be persuaded she (he) will continue to (them) during (his exile) and (after his Return) ommit no occasion of showing Chichelle (particular marks of his Protection) which you'll please (lay before him) with that (prudence which the present circumstances require)

Decemr 11th 1726.

I:

I need not trouble you with a long letter in answer to yours of the 10th Septim, since I think I can do it to your satisfaction in a very few words. I know nothing of any Letters from Mar to the Queen being 332217112910, Manson 18173920 Quintus 1326371022 intercepted ... 28,37231826222526211820ig28, neither do I believe him so so imprudent as to put into writing 29372331, 45223718372327203i, what you say 'tis pretended by some, he did, So I think I need say no more to you on that article.

I never had, Sir, any doubt of Freeman's 28351723261418422010, Honesty ... On the contrary, have of along time had a very great value for him 31355371128, And what was said either by Kennedy or me of the King particular 11263922141723142i9, Persons in the letters which you answer, was chiefly meant for their 39183526372120, information, and as a friendly act, since Mr. Jane the King was very apt to believe that perhaps more was

Cragg'd

First page of a letter from Lord Inverness to Mr Robert Burnet, 11th December 1726; the full text is on pp70 and 72.

Dundas's leaving Holland) without giving me notice of it and the (bad situation) it was represented to me his affairs were (in) which gave me little hopes of his being able to (settle there again) was the reason why I thought it necessary to seek out (a new Correspondent there) and you might have seen at that time how reasonable it was thought that Thomson should have the greatest share of the (choice of the correspondent there thro' whose hands) their (letters) were (to pass). I am heartily glad that (Dundas returned to Holland and) shall be extremely pleased if he can (support himself there) However you need be in no (pain as) to the (person in Rotterdam) thro' whose (hands I sent) the (letters) Laurence (answered) and a small one (thereafter) For tho' he did not know that these (letters came from he yet) I am well informed that he is a very honest man, and one who would not (be suspected in) the (country where he lives) to have such (Dealings which I) thought to be (a great advantage) for I have been often in (pain lest Dundas's) being so (publically known) to be formerly (concerned with the King's affairs) might have occasioned the (opening letters addressed to him in Holland) However I shall for the future when I (write by Holland send my letters to Dundas whose care) and (diligence in such matters) has certainly been (very great) and surely as far as (depends on him) our (correspondence will go very right)

Since the beginning of (Winter we hear of) nothing (but preparations of war) every (where which) are making in some parts (in earnest, If war breaks out) in the (Spring), I hope (our Corrresponence in) this manner shall not be of a very (long standing for matters are) so disposed (that human appearance the King's Interest at home will) be put to (a tryal in case of a Rupture and then) I make no doubt but (our country) will (act its part) and endeavors shall be used to (enable them to do so) In the mean time (all Divisions and personal Differences amongst) those who wish well to (the Kings cause) ought to be (layd aside) as much as possible, which I am persuaded will be Laurence's (great study to bring about) I beg you'll be assured how sincerely I am etc

Issabella (Inverness)

Dear Sir,

I had the honour of yours 13th January which came safely to my hand. Yoy may ashure YourSelf that I should be glad to have an opportunity to serve You, when last together You mocked me when I told you that Warrs would break out, I hope by this time you firmly believe it.

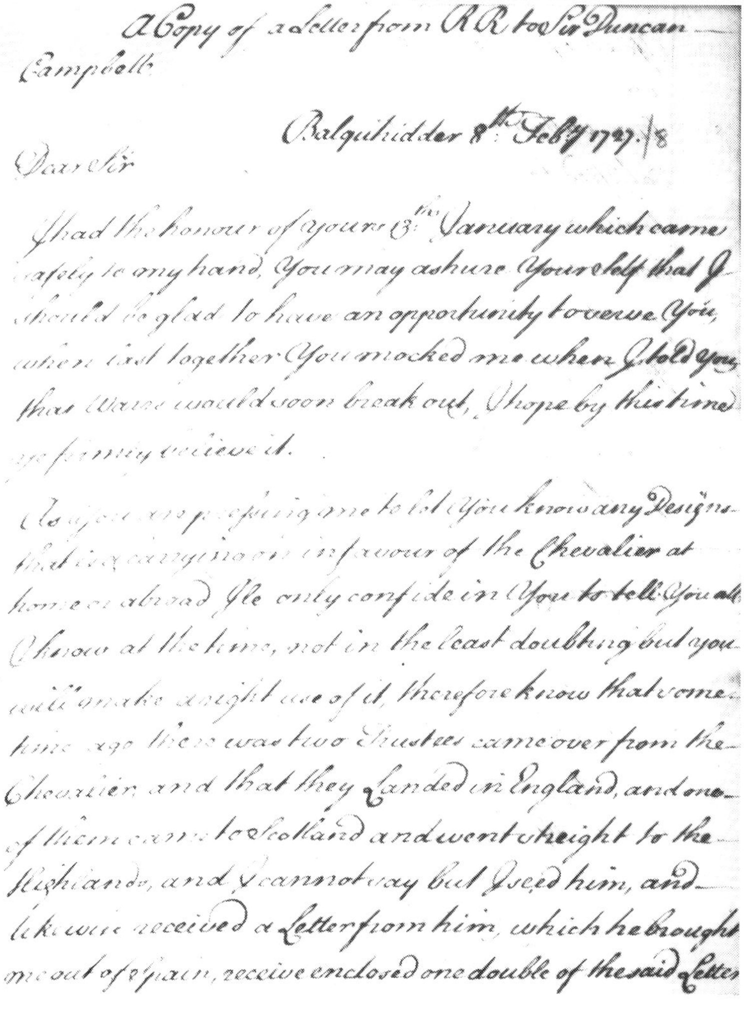

A Copy of a letter from R R to Sir Duncan Campbell

[handwritten letter facsimile]

Extract from a copy of a letter from Rob Roy to Sir Duncan Campbell Balquhidder 8th Feb. 1727–8. Full text on pp72 and 74.

As you are pressing me to let you know any designs that is a carrying on in favour of the Chevalier at home or abroad I'le only confide in You to tell You all I know at the time, not in the least doubting but you will make a right use of it, therefore know that some time ago there was two Trustees came over from the Chevalier and that they landed in England and one of them came to Scotland and went straight to the

73

Highlands and I cannot say but I seed him, and likewise received a letter from him, which he brought me out of Spain, receive enclosed one double of the said letter.

You are pleased to let me understand that I received a letter from a certain Gentleman at London to furnish him with all the Intelligence You could get, I am satisfied to go into any measures you please to propose to me only I may be safe, and not bring myself to any inconvenience thereby, if I'le engage in this affair, I'le go into it overhead and Ears, in the first place I must go straight to the Highlands, and return again to meet the man that has stayed behind in England, He is ordered in his instructions to see me, Although both Gentlemen came over together, yet they have different Instructions, so if I were employed in this affair do you write to London for money, to defray the charges for I am sure it will take a hundred pounds Sterling to do it, if I'le be concerned I will go through every inch of it, I could wish likewise to be so far ashured if I did the Government good service in this affair, that I might promise to myself bread from them in the future, for I need not tell you my narrow circumstances occasioned by all the cross accidents and circumstances of my life if I were encouraged to go in this affair, I'le engage under the penalty of loosing my Life to get full Intellegence of all the Plots and projects, they can contrive or imagine of Landing in this nation, and likewise of any Persons that will go into their measures whic you may understand by the double of the Letter sent You enclos'd whenever You get your return from London I'le wait of You wherever You please to appoint I am.

Sic Sub: Ro Roy Campbell

Dear Rob,

At the writing of this I am drinking your health in good Claret with extraordinary good Company, and there is one of them who would be glad to see You, and You may ashure Yourself that I never missed any opportunity of serving You, You know in my last to you, I told you that our Droving was going on extraordinary well, I have gotten You with the assistance of some others of your friends here to be one of our Company's managers in the Highlands, if you'l not manage to satisfaction, y'el not only ruin Yourself, but also those who have acted for you, there are two gentlemen sent over from our Company to your Company. one of them is your own entire Comrade, who has Your Instructions, this is the

The opening page of a copy of a letter to Rob Roy from Spain.

handsomer (friend?) (send?) that was ever hard for your Highland Droving, providing you'l get them rightly to go into it, if not to Yourselves be it said for my masters Parks will be served without you, but be you sure to keep one thousand good noolt for me and I ashure you to take them off your hand on the first of August next.

(no signiture)

There was one matter of concern to his Norfolk supporters that Townshend took upon himself to look into at this stage. In 1728 he ordered a check into the workings of the 1720 Act which had banned the import of calicoes. It appeared that what had in fact happened was that German linens had come onto the British market, and so the Act, far from helping the English wool manufacturers as had been intended, had provided a protected market for German linen. Townshend's enquiries showed that this was the case, and that English wool manufacturers were no better off. Townshend, however, had resigned before he had time to act on this information.

It was against Townshend's wishes that the Treaty of Seville, bringing together France, Spain and Britain in a treaty of mutual defence, was negotiated. The death of the young French king's regent, the Duc de Bourbon, and his replacement by the Abbé Fleury made the restoration of friendship between France and Spain likely. It was crucial to British policy that France and, if possible, Spain should remain friendly towards Britain if the Jacobites were to be kept without friends in Europe. Although Townshend was nominally in charge of negotiations, it was Robert Walpole, through his brother Horace, the British ambassador in Paris, and a great admirer of Fleury, who was really in control. "Townshend's repugnance to this plan of pacification, was overuled by the prudence and direction of his colleague." The Treaty was finally signed on 29th November 1729, and it was the last act of the administration in which Townshend had a share.

In a final bid to restore his influence, Townshend had set out in May 1729 with the new king, to Hanover. He was the only British minister to go and so hoped to establish his position as sole advisor to George II and Queen Caroline as he had been to George I and the Duchess of Kendal. He hoped to persuade the king to remove the Duke of Newcastle from his position as Secretary of State and replace him with the more pliable Lord Chesterfield. In this Townshend failed. Although a loyal colleague in the past, Newcastle had noticed the weakness in Townshend's position and was now vying for power. Chesterfield had offended the queen and so the king would not approve the appointment. Although the negotiations were supposed to be secret, they were reported to Walpole who realised that the old trust between himself and Townshend was broken.

Townshend, meanwhile, was unable to gain the complete confidence of the king and queen. His illness seems to have left him even more short-tempered than before and once back in England the queen came to prefer Walpole's company and to listen to his views. Arguments between Townshend and Walpole became more and more public. Coxe records an occasion when they met and disagreed over the management of the House of Commons. Townshend conceded that the House of Commons was Walpole's concern, and so would not press his arguments further, but he could not resist a final remark, "but as I now give way, I cannot avoid observing that upon my honour, I think that mode of proceeding would have been most advisable." Walpole then lost his temper and replied "...there is no man's sincerity that I doubt as much as your lordship's." At this Townshend seized Walpole by the collar, both men went for their swords and had to be subdued by their friends.

By the summer of 1729, as the negotiations for the Treaty of Seville were nearly complete, Townshend was ready to resign and wrote to the Bishop of London saying so. As it was Townshend who had been responsible for granting appointments in the Church, it is hardly surprising that the bishop should try and change his mind. His letter to Townshend shows that he understood Townshend's weariness with the affairs of state, but also points out a well-known truth: "I think that your Lordship, who has always been accustomed to business, will feel the want of it and not enjoy that entire ease and satisfaction, you imagine in private life. Any uneasiness we are under for the present, makes us think too favourably of any other situation that may deliver us from them, but things are not the same in speculation as in practice."

During the treaty negotiations, Townshend was at pains to present himself to the king as the only one of the cabinet who supported his Hanoverian interests. He was the only one to share George's fear of Austria and the increasing power of Prussia supported by her. Townshend's correspondence with the King and his notes back suggest that the two were usually in agreement and the King suggested very few alterations to the drafts of letters that Townshend sent him. Frequently they circumvented the Duke of Newcastle and his likely amendments. "If your Majesty approves of the enclosed letter, I will send it privately to Mr (Horace) Walpole, so as the Duke of Newcastle may know nothing of it." While in

Hanover he had concluded an alliance of the four Electors of the Rhineland states against Austria. This was directly against Walpole's wishes as he did not want to anger Austria or do anything that would prevent a reconciliation. However, on their return Walpole gradually gained the support of the queen, who in turn swayed the king away from Townshend's views, and it was in these circumstances that finally, on 16th May 1730, Townshend resigned.

The reasons for the increasing animosity between Townshend and Walpole have been much discussed and there is no doubt that they were rooted in local as well as in national causes. The Townshends had been the leading Norfolk family for many generations and it was difficult for the second Viscount to accept the rise to power of Walpole. When Walpole first went to London, he had been very much Townshend's protégé, but now the situation had changed. In Norfolk, Walpole was replacing his modest country house with a little palace, only to be upstaged later by that of Coke at Holkham. Unlike many a major break between politicians, this one was too much of a personal tragedy for either side to discuss openly. After he resigned, Townshend went to Norfolk and although it is not true to say he never visited London again, he never saw Walpole. He was not prepared to be drawn into any of the opposition groups in Parliament. Walpole was only once persuaded to comment on the end of their long friendship and partnership in government. "It is difficult to trace the causes of a dispute between statesmen, but I will give you the history in a few words – as long as the firm was Townshend and Walpole, the utmost harmony prevailed; but it no sooner became Walpole and Townshend than things went wrong and a separation ensued."

Townshend the Farmer

Although the career of Charles Townshend as a statesman may seem rather inconclusive, there can be no doubt about his achievements and influence as a landlord and agricultural improver. Here, on his own estates, there was no jostling for office; he was served by loyal retainers who treated him with respect and he was totally in control of affairs. His position within the local rural community had been consolidated over generations, and the stability of home contrasted greatly with the ever-shifting sands of the political scene. The years between his retirement from politics in 1730 and his death in 1738 were almost entirely spent at Raynham.

Townshend was living through a period of growing interest in improved farming methods. As literacy was increasing amongst the upper ranks of farmers, more agricultural text books were being produced and there was a lively correspondence between farmers and authors. The period 1640-1750 was a time of falling grain prices, whilst the value of cattle increased by 13 per cent. There was therefore a heightened incentive to improve pasture and find better winter feed. It was against this background that the new grasses and fodder crops spread. Many of the new crops originated in Holland and the first turnips and carrots to be grown in England were grown by Dutch immigrant weavers in closes, or small enclosed fields, near Norwich. Many of the Dutch text books were translated into English, and Norfolk farmers sent their sons to Holland to learn from their Dutch counterparts. East Anglian ties with Holland had always been strong and so Norfolk was ideally placed geographically to receive new ideas. Dutch meadow grasses, such as clover and sainfoin were grown in the region from the 1660s and spread rapidly. Turnips were introduced onto East Anglian farms by 1650, but their popularity spread much more slowly. Although they were probably grown in small quantities on about 50 per cent of East Anglian farms by 1710, they only made up about 9 per cent of the cropped land by 1720; they can hardly be claimed to have played an important part in crop rotations at this date, but it was as a break crop between two cereal plantings that turnips proved to be particularly valuable during the eighteenth century.

Until the development of an alternative, the only way to allow the fields to recover from continuous cereal growing was to leave the land fallow, perhaps opening them to livestock which would forage amongst the weeds. Turnips provided a much more productive solution as they proved to be a very valuable fodder crop which, if fed to livestock on the land, meant the fields could be manured at the same time. Clover and artificial grasses also had a part to play in this new rotation system, providing both nutritious pasture and a good hay crop. Clover was particularly valuable as it replaced the nitrogen in the soil. It was, therefore, possible both to improve the quality of stock and increase the number kept through the winter while at the same time restoring the fertility of the arable for the next cereal crop. By the time Arthur Young visited Norfolk in 1771 "The Norfolk Four-course Rotation" was firmly established. This meant that a cereal crop would be followed by turnips before another cereal was grown. This in turn would be followed by grasses which might well be left for more than one year, depending on the fertility of the soil, before the cycle began again. According to Young the Norfolk system also included enclosure, the use of marl or clay to improve the quality of the land, the creation of large farms and the granting of long leases by the landlords. We shall see how far Townshend was already practising this system more than a generation before Young was writing.

Norfolk was primarily a cereal, particularly a barley growing, area and in a period of falling prices there was a great incentive to increase the efficiency of production. These factors help explain the interest of landowners across Norfolk in agricultural improvement. Families such as the Hobarts at Blickling and the Windhams at Felbrigg, who had added to their wealth through their professional skills as lawyers, brought their business expertise to the running of estates, and this was also true at Raynham by the end of the century.

When Townshend inherited his estates, the agriculture of north-west Norfolk was still mainly practised on open fields and across heaths and commons and these still survived across much of the Raynham estate (see maps pp20–21). It is not surprising therefore that Townshend's interest in the early years was centred on enclosure. There are frequent references in the documents to ditching, hedging, marling and manuring. The area was dominated by an interdependent system of grain and sheep production. The sheep and their dung made the growing of grain, particularly barley, possible. Other manures were also used, such as the very valuable pigeon dung from the dovecotes. In 1709, Townshend ordered the pigeon dung to be spread on some meadows in the park "as an experiment", showing his interest in trying out new ideas.

Normally the sheep were the property of the landlord and we know for instance that Townshend owned sheep at Coxford, Creake, Stiffkey and on the "Great Ground" and "Granoe Hill", Rudham in 1699. The lambs at Creake were sold for £198, so the flock must have been a sizeable one. The sheep would not have been kept only on the open heath, but at certain times of year they would have ranged across the open fields of the tenants. The system was of mutual benefit, providing winter feed for the sheep on the weeds and stubble, whilst manuring the tenants' land ready for the spring sowing. However, there were inevitable clashes of interest between the flock owner and corn grower. The flock owners often wanted to extend the period over which the sheep could be kept in the open fields, whilst the tenants were anxious to consolidate their strips and enclose their land. Enclosure often went hand in hand with the introduction of the new crops which meant land did not have to lie fallow and so provided the tenant with his own winter feed, thus reducing his reliance on the landlord's flock for manuring. Enclosed land that could support a viable mixed farming system with no need for a fallow year, could command a higher rent and so we can see the Townshends taking advantage of a changing situation, giving up their flocks of sheep and relying far more on income from the rents of improved enclosed farms. In 1701 Granoe Hill and Morston fold courses were let, and a 14-year lease for part of Coxford Farm, warren and fold course was granted at an annual rent of £185. The old open fields were broken up into hedged enclosures and marled for continuous cultivation whilst the heaths were enclosed as "outfield" or "brecks" which would be left as pasture and ploughed up only occasionally. Often there was a period of transition when the various types of land use continued side by side. In 1701 "79 acres of infield, and 35 acres in three brecks of the Great Ground foldcourse" were let for £69, while in the same year fold courses, breaks, meadows and pastures are all mentioned in Kipton and all were leased.

Between 1698 and 1701 all but one of the 11 fold courses (for sheep) which had been in hand, were let out to tenants. The fact that wool as well as grain prices were declining during the seventeenth century also encouraged landowners to give up farming on their own account and become instead, rent collectors.

This change in role, from farmer to improving landowner, which had been begun by Charles' father, Horatio, was not achieved without a carefully executed programme of management. Land was exchanged, both between tenants and with other landowners, to consolidate holdings. Much of Townshend's land was already concentrated in two main areas on the light soils of north-west Norfolk, one centred on the two Raynhams where there were already only a few freeholders remaining, and in the area around Stiffkey (see map page 17). The Shipdham and Suffolk estates were at some distance from Raynham and more scattered. They differed from the north Norfolk core in that they were on heavy soils where improvement was difficult before the introduction of piped field drainage in the nineteenth century made the land easier to work.

As more land was bought new enclosed farms were created. For instance, in 1704 a house in Langham was purchased, presumably to provide a base for a newly-created farm. Townshend wrote, "I am very sensible that I suffer extremely from a lack of houses on the estate." Once a holding was enclosed, the land had to be improved. This usually involved the spreading of marl on the light soils to reduce acidity and provide a better soil structure. The marl had to be dug from deep pits and was a winter job which could easily be held up by bad weather as explained by the Reverend Priestland in his letters to Townshend from Raynham in 1713. As well as marling, the new fields had to be hedged and Priestland was busy with this as well. "Little Rainham hedges I question not to get in good order though I have been straightened in time."

Barn at Coxford Abbey Farm. This may well be the barn, the building of which is stipulated in a lease of 1737. The walls contain pieces of dressed stone robbed from the abbey ruins.

New building work also had to be undertaken. Building and repairs were the responsibility of the landlord, amounting to over £500 in many years between 1701 and 1738. In April Priestland wrote, "Robin Tinckler is very pressing for the rebuilding of his barn." In 1737 a 21-year lease was granted for Coxford Abbey Farm. In it Lord Townshend agreed to "Build a barn with four goffsteads (bays) with lean-tos adjoining in the most convenient place on the said farm to be chosen by the tenant and also a rack yard and stack yard adjoining the same farm."

Townshend took a close interest in the farming on the home farm. Not only did he have sheep, but also cattle. In 1704, he instructed Priestland to buy some heifers to graze on the park. He goes on to recommend selective breeding from his best stock; a practice still very much in its infancy. "If any of the calves you mention in your letter are fine ones, breed some of them and dispense of the rest to the best advantage."

Money on the estate always seems to have been very tight. In 1704 Townshend wrote, "I desire you could be as sparing in repairs this year as you can and do nothing but what must be done of necessity, for I would be at as little expense as I can in all things till I have finished my house." Farms were not always easy to let and often in hand. In 1697, for instance, five farms were unlet. On the farms that were leased, tenants were frequently in arrears; the total in many years in the early 1700s was over £2000. In 1705 Townshend wrote, "I am very sorry to hear that money is scarce in Norfolk and that my rents are so ill paid. I shall be put to great inconvenience for want of money for I design to leave (London) the latter end of this month or the first in March. I have several bills to pay and unless you can gather up some money amongst the servants by that time I cannot tell what I shall do."

Samuel Smith was the Bailiff for the estate in the early years of the eighteenth century, but died in 1713, to be replaced by Priestland. In his final year, the accounts had not been well kept and so it was not clear how much money was in fact owed to the estate. "Mr Smith before this audit (September 1713) had taken in very few bills of taxes and repairs of the tenants, which bills, when delivered into Mr Priestland, will lessen the tenants' arrears."

It is not surprising that one of the most important qualities sought in a new tenant was that he should be a man of capital. In recommending a prospective tenant to Lord Townshend in 1713,

Priestland wrote, "I doubt not your lordship will have a good tenant. He (Mr Case) puts his son in, who has married a young woman with £12000 to her fortune, but if it be required, he promises to join with his son for the security of the rent and he is willing to take a long lease, for life if you please."

It is clear from the remaining correspondence and papers at Raynham that the estate was efficiently run, but this in itself would not be enough to account for Townshend's fame.

Even before he died in 1738, Townshend's reputation as an improving landowner was well established and his encouragement of the growing of turnips was proverbial, although exactly what he did to deserve this title is obscure. Alexander Pope, in his Imitations of Horace, the second epistle of the second book, published in 1734, wrote of two brothers; one was hard working while,

> *"The other slights for Women, Sports and Wines*
> *All Townshend's turnips and all Grosvenor's Mines"* (lines 272–3)

By the time Arthur Young visited Norfolk at the end of the eighteenth century Townshend's fame was described in agricultural books throughout Europe. "The name of this Lord Townshend is repeated with an increase of applause and eulogy for his agriculture, by writers, and relished by whole nations of readers who scarcely know an iota of his political life." Young believed it was Townshend who had introduced turnips to Norfolk, but did not think he was the first person to marl. We know now that turnips were grown in small quantities for a generation before Townshend, but there may be more truth in Young's next statement; "He (Townshend) certainly practised the turnip culture on such an extent and with such success, that he was copied by all his neighbours." The earliest reference to turnips in a lease is in 1697 when John Butler of East Rudham was required in his last year to sow "turnapps" on newly enclosed land, leaving them well fenced in on his departure. From the following year some leases specifically mention the cultivation of turnips in a rotation with other crops. One lease for 18 years allows the tenant to take two crops of turnips and four crops of corn from 40 acres of outfield while leaving the area under grass for the remaining years of the lease. In 1698 Robert Tinckler of East Rudham committed himself to divide Thorn Close into 3 enclosures and sow one of them with turnips every year.

The examples of leases mentioning turnips increase throughout the period. For instance in the 1720s, Abel Brett agreed to leave 60 acres of his 754-acre farm at Toftrees in clover and 100 acres ready to be sown with turnips in the last year of his lease. These specific references to turnips in leases are far earlier than on any other Norfolk estate and show that here at least, they were more than a small experimental fodder crop, but were recognised for their value in a rotation. Whether they were as yet being fed to animals in the fields or simply to stall-fed cattle is not made clear. If leases were being obeyed, the acreage of turnips and clover grown on the Raynham estate would have increased greatly in the first twenty years of the eighteenth century.

Like his father, Townshend was a great believer in leases as a way to improve farming on his estates, and they become more exact in their stipulations in the years following his retirement from politics. As early as the 1650s, Horatio was granting leases, some stipulating in detail how the land was to be farmed. One granted to C Perkins in 1663 stated that the land should be ploughed "in course", the muck and compost produced on the farm should be spread back on the land, no new land was to be ploughed up and the duty of "day work" on repairs was to be observed. After 1730 they frequently stipulate how much manure and marl should be spread and how many pounds of grass seed should be sown per acre. At their simplest, the leases state that the dung and manure should be kept on the farm, two crops of grain should not be grown in succession but clover or rye-grass should be grown in between and old meadows should not be broken up. The fact that the precise terms of leases varied from farm to farm suggests that they were individually negotiated to suit the land on each farm, and the most likely person to have worked out the terms was Townshend himself. It may be argued that these very restrictive leases prevented experiment and innovation on the part of the tenant, but sometimes the farmer was allowed more freedom. Robert Seppings at Coxford Abbey was "at liberty to sow what clover and other grass seeds he shall think proper upon any of the land sown with summer corn this year."

However, not all leases were as progressive. The terms of a 21-year lease for a farm in Stiffkey granted in 1739 were presumably circumscribed by local conditions. It stated that only two corn crops should be grown in succession and that the unenclosed land "must be farmed according to the custom and usage of Stiffkey."

Arthur Young also credits Townshend with the enclosure and hedging on much of his estate and this is supported by the evidence of the estate records. "The fields are of a proper size for farms of between 300 and 800 acres, they are square, well disposed in relation to the home stall, the roads and the soil; all are admirably fenced, in as great perfection as any hedges of the present time." As Young's visit was only 50 years after Townshend's death, it is very likely that his observations are correct. Figures for expenditure survive for the years 1706-1729 and although the annual figure is very variable, it is frequently over £100 for hedging.

The commitment of tenants to improvement was ensured by the granting of long leases. In Horatio's day, large farms were often held on long leases. 40 per cent were for ten years or more, whilst 50 per cent were for seven years or less. After 1708 leases were often for from 17 to 21 years and sometimes for life. With this degree of security Townshend hoped that tenants would be prepared to risk their own capital on improvements.

It is perhaps because of his leases that Townshend became so famous. By the end of the eighteenth century long leases containing detailed husbandry clauses were an accepted part of good estate management, but in the early eighteenth century they were certainly ahead of their time. On the neighbouring Holkham estate, for instance, rather general leases are found from the late 1690s, but it is not until the 1720s that artificial grasses are mentioned, and in the 1730s, turnips.

One of the inevitable results of Townshend's programme of enclosure and consolidation to create large farms was the reduction in the number of small tenants. In the parishes of Langham and Morston there was one farm valued at £90, one at £56, and 25 at under £50 in 1701. By 1750, there were two over £100, two between £50 and £100 and only nine under £50. Similarly in Stibbard and Ryburgh there was one farm valued at £45, one at £30 and seven under £10 in 1701 and only one paying £160 in rent by 1756. This compares with the Holkham estate where in 1727, 26 farms were let for over £100 a year and one over £300.

Coupled with this increase in the size of farms was a great increase in the estate's value and Townshend judged his own success in financial terms. In 1732, he boasted to the Earl of Oxford that by marling, enclosing and sowing turnips, he had increased his income by £900 per annum. The total rental in 1701 was £3725; by 1730 this had risen to £6048 and in 1756 it was £8180. It is not clear how this increase was achieved. It was undoubtedly partly due to new purchases, but unfortunately it is not possible to calculate the exact acreage of the estate at different dates. It was also partly the result of increasing rents on land already owned by the enclosure of old heath and common, allowing new land to come into cultivation; of consolidation of farms and the ending of scattered strips; and the improvement of the land by marling and careful farming.

After 1730, Townshend was able to devote more time to his interest in experimentation, which his political career had prevented him pursuing. There is a note of regret in a letter written to Thomas Ward while he was abroad between 1709 and 1711 in which he says, "I have little time to think of my country affairs." Once back permanently in Norfolk, he became far more involved, receiving his rents personally from his tenants and helping them find the best market for their corn. It was through these discussions and contacts as well as through his efforts at reorganising the farmland on his estates that his influence would have been felt.

There can be no doubt that when Townshend died in 1736, he left a well-managed estate to his son. Gone was the fold course system of agriculture where large flocks of sheep, usually owned by the landlord, roamed the heaths and commons. Most of this land, along with the open fields had been enclosed and divided into large compact farms of regularly marled fields. These were let on long leases with detailed husbandry clauses encouraging progressive agriculture. Rotations, which included fodder crops of turnips and improved grasses between cereals were being implemented and as a result the value of the estate had risen drastically. All the changes which Arthur Young described as being typical of the "Norfolk System" were to be found at Raynham 50 years before he made his first tour of Norfolk.

The farms were well placed to benefit from the increasing price of grain through the eighteenth century. All this provided a shining example to neighbouring landlords and farmers a couple of generations before agricultural improvement was made fashionable by, amongst others, "Coke of Holkham" and "Farmer George" (King George III).

Townshend the Man

History remembers Townshend primarily as a great agricultural improver, and in this it is fully justified. His political career presents a rather confused picture and it is even more difficult to be clear about his personality and character. There are few personal papers surviving and so we must rely on the often very biased opinions of others as well as the evidence of Townshend's own actions.

He is described as a "handsome, burly man" and this is borne out in the surviving portraits. Unlike Walpole, who was renowned for his eloquence, Townshend was said to be a poor public speaker. He was a regular attender at the House of Lords, first speaking in 1701, and frequently contributing thereafter. His concern for detail meant that his speeches were often cumbersome and long winded. Lord Chesterfield described him as "inelegant in his language, often perplexed in his arguments, but always speaking sensibly and with a thorough knowledge of his subject."

The one trait in his character about which all, including Townshend himself, were agreed, was that he was very short-tempered and did not suffer fools gladly. In this, as in so many other ways, he took after his father, who, although able, energetic and industrious, was said to be aggressive and overbearing, refusing to

West front Raynham Hall

88

consider contrary opinions. He died when Charles was still a child but seems to have passed on many of his characteristics all the same.

The few personal papers that do survive suggest that Charles expected efficient and instant service from those who provided for his needs and the caustic notes that passed between his valet and suppliers in London have already been quoted. Nor were his bursts of temper confined to domestic matters. At court and in dealing with affairs of state, he could be equally irascible. His temper was even a joking matter between himself and Walpole in the early years of their friendship, when a little teasing was permissible. Lord Hervey described him as "a slave to his passions... He was rash in his undertakings, violent in his proceedings, haughty in his carriage, brutal in his expression and cruel in his disposition." All of these faults would surely have made him very unsuited to the diplomatic missions with which he was entrusted. Add to this the slowness with which he came to decisions, and having reached them, his dogged refusal to change his mind, it is surprising that he was trusted with foreign affairs for so long. Although his concern for detail may have helped in the delicate negotiations, both with Scotland over the Act of Union, and at The Hague, there is no doubt that in some of his decisions,

East front Raynham Hall

such as the terms of the Barrier Treaty, he showed bad judgement. The only explanation for his continued ability to remain in control of foreign affairs is that suggested by Lord Hervey. "He had been so long in business that, notwithstanding his slow blundering capacity, he might have got through the routine of his employment... with only moderate abilities, he had boundless confidence in his own capacity to play a principal part in the continental drama."

Lord Hervey was no friend of Townshend and his long damning description of his failings ignores qualities that were very unusual in a statesman of this period.

Firstly, he was said, in great contrast to Walpole, to have made no money, beyond his official salary, from his government appointments. His integrity was never questioned and, in an age when government was riddled with corruption, this was truly remarkable.

Secondly, he was a loyal family man on whom no scandal could ever be pinned. He was devoted to both his wives, and as we have seen, his family often accompanied him on diplomatic missions. He refused to take up his appointment as Lord Lieutenant of Ireland and move to Dublin because of his "domestic affairs".

He had a large family. His first wife, Elizabeth Pelham, whom he married in 1698, bore him five children, before her death in 1711. Two years later he married Dorothy Walpole, who had six children before she died in 1726. It is clear that he was never happier than on his estates and surrounded by his family. No doubt his success as a landowner and farm improver was because it was here that he felt most at home. He could be at ease away from the intrigues of Court.

Alexander Pope commented that his favourite subjects for conversation centred around rural improvement, and particularly, the importance of turnips. In this Townshend was ahead of his time. It was not until the next generation that improving one's estates became the fashionable activity and subject of conversation for the landed classes. It is, therefore, even more surprising that he should doggedly hold on to office, rather than retire quietly to his estates.

Perhaps it was his conscientiousness and sense of duty that kept him at a job to which he appears to have been so temperamentally unsuited. No doubt he feared for the security of Britain which, left in the hands of Walpole, he thought would take second place to the economic retrenchment he favoured.

The years after his retirement may well have been his happiest. At Raynham he was surrounded by loyal retainers, and his local status in his community, as Lord Lieutenant, was never questioned. Members of his family still held local parliamentary seats, and so he was in touch with what was going on. He had time to indulge his interest in horses, through racing and hunting, both

Corridor vista in the east front, showing the doorway pediments designed by William Kent (Copyright A F Kersting)

over his own park and farms and those of his neighbours. He had always been a keen follower of the hounds and had spent much time hunting when with the king in Hanover.

He had always maintained his interest in the more cultural pursuits of the gentry, developed both at Cambridge and in Italy. He enjoyed art, music, classics and history and now had time to

The marble hall, again designed by Kent (Copyright A F Kersting)

appreciate the elegant neo-classical interior of his house, created for him at Raynham by William Kent, as well as his pictures and library.

Although he spent most of his time at Raynham, he did occasionally travel, visiting Bath in 1733. The sum of £48.14s.7d. is recorded as being the total cost of the trip. Whether he went for medical or social reasons is not recorded, but he certainly remained active until his sudden death, resulting from an apoplectic fit, or a stroke, in 1738.

In his last years he was able to devote himself to the task for which he has remained justly famous: the improvement of his estate and its agriculture. There is no doubt that as much as two generations before Coke of Holkham, Townshend was advocating the growing of turnips and grasses to replace the fallow year, and writing these improvements into leases. Unlike, Coke, he did not have a famous agent, and so we must assume that he was always very much in control even before he retired to his estates and was able to take a more personal interest in the success of these changes. It was on his farms and his estates rather than in the House of Lords and London, that his interests and talents were shown, and it was here that he laid the foundations for "The Norfolk System" which was to be made famous through the writings of Arthur Young and the publicity stunts of Coke at nearby Holkham. It is to the pioneering work of "Turnip" Townshend that the "Agricultural Revolution" of the late eighteenth century must trace its roots.

Index

Act of Union with Scotland (1707) 35,46,89
agriculture (general) 17-25, 79-87 (see also under specific entries)
Algeria 53
Andrews, Robert 45
Anne, Queen 34,35,36,37, 40,43,47
army 37,45,53
Ashe, Sir John, father of Mary Townshend 28
Ashe, Mary, wife of Horatio Townshend 28
Astley family of Melton Constable 8
Atterbury, Francis, Bishop of Rochester 43,56
Austria 46,47,48,61,62,77
Aylsham 55

Bacon family of Stiffkey 8,16
Bacon, Walter, MP for Norwich 35
Balliol College 48,50,59
barns 41,83
Barrier Treaties 39,40,47, 48, 49,90
Belgium 39,47,48,62
Berndorf 48
Blairgowry 46
Blenheim, Battle of (1704) 37
Blickling 11,12,80
Bolingbroke, Viscount St John Henry 43,44,45
Bothmar, J G von 43,51
Bourbon, Duc de 76
Bremen, Germany 48
Brett, Abel of Toftrees 85
Broglio, Count 59
Brown, Captain 64
Butler, John of Rudham 84
Buxton family of Heydon 8

Cabinet Council 36,63
calico 15,76
Calthorpe, Thomas 28,30
Cambridge 25,30
Campbell, Sir Duncan 64,73
Caroline (Queen of George II) 64-5,70
carrots 79
Cartaret, John Earl Granville 45, 58,59
Castleman, Mr 45-6
Castle Rising 9,34
cattle 79,83,85
Chambers, John, MP for Norwich 35
Charles II 7,16,30

Charles XII of Sweden 48
Chester, Mr 46
Chesterfield, Philip Dormer Stanhope, 4th Earl of 76,88
church 53,77
cloth industry 14,54,76
clover 14,79,80,85
Cokes of Holkham 8,87,93
commons/heaths 12,14, 19-22, 80,87
Compton, Sir Spencer, Earl of Wilmington 64
Cornwall 45,46
Coxe, William 28,77
Coxford 17,18,22,41,81, 82,83 ,85
Creake 17,81

De Grey family of Merton 8
Denmark 48,49,61
Devon 46
ditching 80
dovecote 80-1
Dutch (see Holland)
Dyer, Mr 45

East India Company 30
Edinburgh 56,60
education 29
elections 41-2
enclosure 24,80-1,86,87
Eton 25,28

fallow 80,93
Felbrigg 12,80
Flanders (see Belgium)
Fleury, Abbé 76
fold courses 25,81,87
Forster, Thomas 46
France
    Terms for peace 37-40
    Jacobites 45,46-7,48
    policy towards 49,50, 56-7, 62,64

Garter, Order of the 59-60
George I 9,43,44,47,48,49,51, 57,58,59,61,63,73-4
George II, and Prince of Wales 49,51,52,59,64-5,76-7
Gibraltar 61
Glensheil, Scotland 63
Glorious Revolution 7
Godolphin, Earl of Sidney 40
grain 79,80,81,85
"Grand Alliance" 37
"Grand Tour" 25,30

Hague, The 36,38,48,50,89
Hamilton, Douglas William, Duke of 56
Hamilton, George 46
Hanover 48,49,51,52, 57,58,59,61,64,76-7,92

Hanover, Treaty of (1725) 61
Harbord family of Gunton 8
hedging 80,81,86
Helhoughton 19,21,23
Hervey, Lord John 89-90
Heydon 12-13
Highlands of Scotland 63
Hobart family of Blickling 12,80
Holkham 16,60,86,87,93
Holland 36,39,46,47, 48,49,51,53,60,61,79
Holland, John, of Quidenham 35
Hookeath, Mr 45
Hoste family of Sandringham 9
Houghton 16,28,60
House of Commons 9,54, 62,77
House of Lords 30,34, 54,88,93
hunting 91-2

Inverness 71,72
Ireland 46,52,90
Islay, Archibald Campbell, Earl of 60-1
Italy 30

Jacobites 34,42,44-6,47,48, 52,55-7,60,63-4,65-75
James II (and VII) 7,35,43
James III (and VII, the "Old Pretender") 35,43,44,45,46,55, 56,57,60,65,66,68,73-4
Jones, Inigo 25
"Junta" 35,36,38,40

Kendal, Duchess of 58,59,76
Kent, William 27,60,93
Kings Lynn 9,15,35

Langham 16,19,82,86
Layer, Christopher 55,56
leases 83,84,85,86,87,93
Leith, Scotland 63
LeStrange, Edward 30,41
linen 76
London 33,45,46,54,60,63, 83,89,93
London, Bishop of 77
Lord Lieutenant 10,16,46,91
Louis XIV 49
Lovat, Lord 53

Mar, John Erskine, Earl of 46, 56,63
Marlborough, John Churchill, first Duke of 36,37,38,40
manuring 80,81,85
marling 41,50,82,87
Morston 16,19,86

navy 48
Netherlands (see Belgium)
Newcastle, Thomas Pelham
    Holles, Duke of 59,76,77
Norfolk 54,63,76,78,79,80,
    84,87
Norfolk, Dukes of 7
"Norfolk husbandry" 7,80,93
Norris, Sir John 48
Northern War 48,50,52
Norway 61
Norwich 9,14

open-field system 7,12,80-1,87
Oriel College, Oxford 46
Orleans, Duke of 49
Ormonde, James Butler, second
    Duke of 45
Osnabruck, Bishop of 64
Ostend Company 61
Oxburgh Hall 12
Oxford, Earl of 54,86
Oxford University 45
Oxnead 12
Oxwick 17

Paris 62,76
parliamentary elections 9,41-2
Paston family of Oxnead 8
Pattesley 17
Pelham, Elizabeth, first wife of
    Charles Townshend
    31,32,90
Perth, Scotland 46
Peterhead, Scotland 46
petitions 52-3
Philip V of Spain 49
Pointz, Stephen 50
Poland 48
Pope, Alexander 83,89
Portugal 62
Preliminaries of Paris (1727) 61
Presbyterians 35,46
Preston 46
Pretender (see James III & VIII)
Prideaux, Edmund 27,32
Priestland, the Rev 41,83-4
Privy Council 36
Prussia 75-6

Raynham estate 25,27,79,80,
    83,84
Raynham Hall 12,25-7,32,60,
    88,89,91-2
Raynham parishes 16,19,20-1,
    22,24,82
Regency, Council of 43
rents 24,25,41-2,83,87
"Rob Roy" Macgregor of
    Balquidder, Scotland
    63-4,72-4
Roman Catholics 35,46
Rudham 17,21,41,81,84

Russia 48,50,53,57,58,61,62
Ryburgh 86

sainfoin 99
Scarborough, Earl of 59
Schaub, Sir Luke 57
Scotland 35,46,60,63
Scott, Sir Walter 63
Secretary of State 43,44,
    54,57,59,76
Seppings, Robert of Coxford
    Abbey 85
Seville, Treaty of, 1729 76,77
shackage 12,14,25
sheep farming 12,17,80-1,87
sheep walks 12
Shereford 17,25
sheriff 10
Shipdham 16,82
Sinclair, Captain 63
Smith, Samuel 41,83
Somers, Baron John 38
South America 39
South Creake (see Creake)
South Sea Bubble 55,57
Spain 37,48,49,57,61,62
Stanhope, James, first Earl of
    44,48,49,50,51,52,53,54
Stibbard 41,86
Stiffkey 16,19,81,82,85
Stiffkey Hall 13,19
Strachan, John 64
strip fields 19,20,21,22,23,24,
    80-1,87
Suffolk 16,82
Sunderland, Charles Spencer,
    3rd Earl of 40,51,54,55
Sweden 48,49,57,58

Tatterset 24
tenant farms 12,19,24-5, 41-2,
    81,83-4,86-7
Thetford 9
Tinckler, Robert of Rudham 84
Toftrees 17,18,85
Torcy, Duc de 37
Tories 34,40,42,43,44,47,54,55
Townshend, Horatio 8,10,16,
    82,85,86,88-9
Townshend, Sir Roger 25
trade 52
Treasury, First Lord of 40,54
Turks 53
Turner, John 35
turnips 14,79,84,85,87,93

Utrecht, Treaty of 42,43,54

Verdun 48

Wade, General 63
Walpole, Dorothy, second wife
    of Charles Townshend 28,
    42,62,90

Walpole, Horace 28,38,40,43,
    49,57,62,76
Walpole, Col Robert 28
Walpole, Robert
    early years 28
    enters House of
    Commons 34
    fall from power 40
    Paymaster General 44
    dismissal (1717) 52
    in opposition 54
    First Lord of the Treasury 54
    conflict with Townshend
    58,60, 61,76,78
    and George II 64
Walpole family 8,9
Ward, Thomas 30
Waterford, Ireland 52
weaving 14-15,79
Whigs 9,30,38,39,43,44,47,48
William III and Mary II 7,34
Windham family of Felbrigg
    8,80
Wodehouse family of
    Kimberley 8
wool 76
Worcester College, Oxford 46

Yarmouth 9
Young, Arthur 80,84,86,87,93

Select Bibliography

ALLISON, K J *"The sheep-corn husbandry of Norfolk in the 16th and 17th centuries"*, *Agricultural History Review vol 5, 1957*

COXE, Archdeacon William *Memoirs and Life of Robert Walpole 2 vols (1798)*

Memoirs and life of Horatio (Lord) Walpole (1802)

DEFOE, Daniel *A tour through the Eastern Counties of England, 1722 (1724)*

FRITZ, Paul S *The English ministers and Jacobitism between the rebellions of 1715 and 1745 (1975)*

HILL, Brian W *Sir Robert Walpole (1989)*

HILL, Oliver & CORNFORTH, John *English Country Houses Caroline 1625-1685 (1966)*

HOLMES, G *British politics in the reign of Queen Anne 2nd ed, (1987)*

HORN, D B *Great Britain and Europe in the 18th century (1967)*

JONES, J R *Country and Court England 1658-1714 (1978)*

KETTON CREMER, R W *Norfolk Portraits (1946)*

Norfolk Gallery (1947)

Norfolk Assembly (1957)

Norfolk in the Civil War (1969)

MINGAY, G E *English Landed Society in the 18th century (1963)*

MOORE, A W *Norfolk and the Grand Tour (1985)*

OVERTON, M *"The diffusion of agricultural innovation in early modern England. Turnips and clover in Norfolk and Suffolk 1580-1740"* *Transactions of the Institute of British Geographers Vol 10(1985)*

PARKER, R A C *Coke of Norfolk, a financial and agricultural study, 1707-1842 (1975)*

PEVSNER, N B L *North-east Norfolk and Norwich (Buildings of England, 1962)*

North-west and South Norfolk (Buildings of England, 1962)

PLUMB, J H *Sir Robert Walpole 2 vols. (1956 & 1960)*

ROSENHEIM, J M *The Townshends of Raynham (1989)*

SPECK, W A *Stability and Strife England 1714-1760 (1977)*